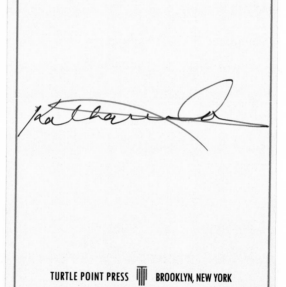

TURTLE POINT PRESS ▐▐▐ BROOKLYN, NEW YORK

Delighting Writers and Readers for Thirty Years, 1990–2020

The Stranger I Become

On Walking, Looking and Writing

KATHARINE COLES

TURTLE POINT PRESS *Brooklyn, NY*

Requests for permissions to make copies of any part of the work
should be sent to:
Turtle Point Press, 208 Java Street, Fifth Floor, Brooklyn, NY, 11222
info@turtlepointpress.com

Library of Congress Catalogue-in-Publication Data
Names: Coles, Katharine, author.
Title: The Stranger I Become: On Walking, Looking,
and Writing / Katharine Coles.
Identifiers: LCCN 2021008814 | ISBN 9781885983862 (paperback)
Subjects: LCGFT: Essays.
Classification: LCC PS3553.O47455 S77 2021 | DDC 814/.6--dc23
LC record available at https://lccn.loc.gov/2021008814

The author would like to thank the following publications, in which some of
the essays previously appeared, sometimes in slightly different form:
Axon (Australia): "In the Way of Knowing." Crazyhorse: "Filament."
New Writing (UK): "The Poetics of Distraction" and "Lens." Text
(Australia): "The Stranger I Become" and "My Objects of Affection." "Lens"
was reprinted in The Science of the Story (Bloomsbury, 2019).

Cover design by Alban Fischer
Layout and typesetting by Martha Ormiston

Paperback ISBN: 978-1-885983-86-2
eBook ISBN: 978-1-885983-95-4

Printed in the United States of America
First Edition

I do not know
the man so
bold
He dare in lonely
Place –
That awful
stranger –
Consciousness
Deliberately
face –

EMILY DICKINSON

Contents

Author's Note   11

THE STRANGER I BECOME   13

THE POETICS OF DISTRACTION (a defense)   31

LENS   41

IN THE WAY OF KNOWING   51

FILAMENT   63

REFLECT   77

HOW ARE YOU FEELING   89

BLIND SPOT   97

MY OBJECTS OF AFFECTION   111

Sources   133

Permissions   139

Acknowledgments   141

About the Author   143

for
William Jeffery Coles

October 31, 1929 – February 16, 2020

Author's Note

For this collection, I have transcribed Dickinson's poems directly from the handwritten manuscripts in the Emily Dickinson Archive, preserving breaks as they appear in the originals, rather than using the versions in the Franklin or Johnson editions. Where lines are quoted within the text, I have indicated breaks that appear in the archival but not the print versions with "|" instead of "/". Readers can access the handwritten facsimiles themselves through the links provided on the Sources page.

THE STRANGER I BECOME

for Jen Webb

Walking is good for thinking,
but not vice versa.

SHARON BRYAN, "USE CAPRICIOUS
IN A SENTENCE"

I am known to walk a lot by modern standards, on most days for seven or more miles. Fitness isn't the point, at least not all of it. About goats, Sharon Bryan tells us, "They keep their balance/by staying in motion"—and balance isn't all physical, at least for me. Walking spins ideas free; its rhythm puts me in touch with myself, and the distance I travel reminds me I am always loose on the planet. Setting a pace, sallying forth, re-minds me, mind comprising as it does every part of my body, skin, eyes, ears, and, not least, my heart, which tells me I am frightened or in love before I know to ask. My senses, not my brain, create the ongoing sense of change I know as "mind." Without my moving body, my brain would be a dull grey blob, inert. Like it or lump it.

Walking enacts this change and its constancy. Philosophers have Heidelberg's Philosophenweg, or Philosopher's Walk, which is open also to physicists and mathematicians, many of whom are great walkers, and even to poets. You can reach it from Heidelberg Station on foot if you're willing to walk forty minutes or so through the less picturesque suburbs to get there. From it you can contemplate the ruined castle on the other side of the valley, and consider how destruction comes to all bodies, often so slowly we don't notice.

~

Before I thought much about dissolution, when I was still a young poet, I worked toward unity, trying to develop a poetic voice, which I believed would distinguish me. I didn't realize that I was also working to fit in, to give the community of poets a handle to grab, a way to say, Yes, this is *a poet*, a creature whose vocalizations we recognize *as lyric*. I wanted to appear at once new and familiar, wild and domesticated. I wanted to teach myself how to write a poem—how to *want* to write a poem, an essay, any piece at all—that was, as the fashion demanded, about only one thing.

Now, on days when I have too much work to do or the world outside is covered, as this morning, in snow, I walk on a treadmill facing a glass wall looking out over treetops into a canyon. I walk, in other words, toward the edge of a cliff, only a few feet in front of me, an edge that never arrives.

Still, the earth spins. The canyon falls toward the house through Gambel oak at the front and away at the back into wildland. On this shortest day I can hear the frantic predawn singing of coyotes circling their prey. Once, on RadioLab, I heard a biologist claim—adamantly—that reports of people hearing coyotes singing to each other are false. He does not have a plausible explanation for exactly what else we might be hearing (Dogs? The howls of our hungry hearts?) or why we would universally identify these calls as belonging to coyotes if they don't. Still, our claims remain *unverified*, as he says, his voice querulous. Perhaps he imagines us plunging into some mass hallucination, all our unscientific minds, made irrational by winter dark, casting us back into a time not so long ago when we still knew we are prey.

~

For example, the other day, at dusk, I opened my front door to a slightly crazy-eyed pizza delivery man. He was new, and he had just walked for the first time down our long, steep driveway under deepening winter shadow and native trees interplanted with apples. We leave the fruit for deer who live in the gully running down the hillside next to the house. That evening, the apples long since eaten, they huddled in the clearing on the other side of the carport, holding so still you had to know they were there to see them.

He asked, "Do you have wild dogs in the neighborhood?"

Me? I laughed and cocked an ear. I have never, in this neighborhood, seen a feral dog, much less had one. I see coyotes all the time, I told him, and even more frequently hear their calls. I pointed at the front walk behind him. The first week we lived in our house, I said, I was standing by the window when a lactating female strolled along it as if she owned the place. Like the time I shared a long gaze with a mountain lion not ten feet in front of me, our look measuring out a much greater than physical distance between us, I was riveted in place, my spine alive with its own electricity.

"Coyotes," he said, and relaxed. He didn't want to think ordinary dogs, the kind he knows and takes into his home, could sound like that. And the truth is, that biologist notwithstanding, they don't, not that I've heard, slide eerie voices up and down a scale tuned to another key, singing out freedom and their hunger. You don't have to be a scientist to know this. Even calling back to coyotes, as I've heard my dogs do, frantic with fear and excitement, they sound like themselves.

This morning, when I went up to get the paper, I saw in the light snow next to my car a large paw print, canid, enacting absence-in-presence: *I was here*.

~

As the sun rises, finches flutter up from the oaks' shelter by the score to peck at feeders my husband, Chris, keeps full. He changes out types of seed, blocks of suet and insects, and, in the summer, sugar water and orange halves dabbed with grape jelly to attract birds coming through in waves as the seasons change. The small birds draw hawks, which ride the canyon updrafts into the sky or plummet over the roof, sometimes just a few feet away from where I startle at their swift appearances. Occasionally a weasel or fox wanders through, or a lone, elusive bobcat stalking the raccoons our feeders also draw, and once, years ago, a moose, gigantic in snow-lit dark, who paused to strip the bark from the aspens out front.

I don't notice every such event, even when I am awake and facing it squarely. Chris installed a mount for my laptop on the treadmill, and over time I have learned to type at four miles per hour and read at seven, if the reading is easy. I can compose syllabi while walking, or grade papers, or mark up dissertations, or answer the constant stream of anxious emails from students. As you might guess, I don't get carsick either, thank goodness, or airsick, or seasick. But when I do raise my eyes from the screen and cast my gaze beyond the glass, I move not only out of my room, familiar and disorganized for my sole convenience, but out of myself.

The canyon, along with its bird population, changes season by season. The screech owls that returned to our nesting box in the fall will fledge chicks by June and scatter into summer darkness. The snow covering everything now in its great blankness will give way to melt and detail, then to buds and leaves that will eventually flame and fall, to grasses that will emerge in soft green then go gold and dry to tinder as fire season arrives. Changes occur not only seasonally: hour by hour, even moment by moment, the light that defines this landscape shifts and slants, brightens and shadows, drags its bright tail across the mountains. Every time I follow my eyes outward, then, I am transported—not only out of my own head, which can forget that its very machinations make it alien to itself, but also into a place made constantly new by the turn of the planet.

Of course, I prefer to walk outside, where it is harder to sink into myself. I walk often into the foothills out back and sometimes into stranger wildlands, but most intentionally through cities and their adjacent or internalized "natural," by which I mean humanly remodeled, landscapes. When every summer I visit London for a conference in Kensington, I book a hotel at least three miles away. For years, I stayed at the creaky old Academy in Gower Street, making my way in the morning foot traffic along one of those London streets that keeps changing its name—Goodge to Mortimer to Wigmore—and finally down into Hyde Park and Kensington Gardens. I found the shortest footpath through the woods; when I had time, I stopped on the bridge over the Serpentine and watched the swans admire their reflections in the water. Returning in the evening, I might brave Piccadilly and the teeming theater district with its brilliant marquees.

More recently, I've discovered a strenuously modern hotel in South Bank. From there, the walk takes me along the river and across Westminster Bridge, under Big Ben, and up St. James Park on the Birdcage Walk. The trick is not to arrive at the palace gates during the changing of the guards, when the crush of tourists makes passage into Green Park all but impossible and is sure to make me late. Either way, I love emerging from under trees and bird song into an urban mix of shops, restaurants, statues of figures whose names I may or may not know, even crowds.

As Calvino reminds us, an imaginary city haunts every real one, and vice versa. When I anticipate traveling to a city I have visited before, or when I am walking through it again, at least three versions of it inhabit the same space. I carry my memory, my imagination, my desire—all interpenetrated and interrupted by the sounds, smells, and sights before me: a new restaurant, a scarlet-painted door I don't remember noticing before though I have walked this Mayfair street a dozen times, each detail in its moment either committed to or lost to memory, often not for the first time. Of course, the passers-by, the faces and fashions and conversations, change every time; on a crowded pavement, even if I pass the same person twice, unless we have some reason to speak I probably won't remember.

Don't mistake me. I don't lament the provisionality of cities, of the world or universe, even of memory. I travel out as I travel into myself, seeking to be unmoored. Just now, walking my own treadmill in my own small western city, I am anticipating Philadelphia, Washington, D.C. (in two versions), London again, Frankfurt, Montreal, Canberra, Winchester, Paris—all on my calendar, all remembered, made up, folded in their own emergent realities. Even the details I remember will not, when I encounter them again, be as I thought.

On my treadmill, looking out, I would never know that, just as the canyon falls away before me, behind me, unrolling in the other direction from the top of the foothill at the top of my drive, lies a city covered, today, in snow—downtown less than two miles away, the university three. I live exactly on the interface, on the edge of a neighborhood that plummets on one side into wilderness, on the other into an urban heart.

This is my own city—dusty, western, with wide streets and low buildings. I know it so well I forget to see it; even on my treadmill, on the streets of Jakarta or London, on a glacier in Antarctica, forgetting it, I keep it in mind. It lives in me and beyond me. Like every other city, it remains a mystery.

~

Perhaps the more recognizable one's voice is as participating in the poetics of the moment, the less recognizably it belongs uniquely to oneself. This is the tension the artist faces. I think how Emily Dickinson's nominal adherence to common measure allows us to think of her as occupying a certain category—call it "maiden poet"— when she is on examination entirely strange, *hors catégorie*, set loose from time. Frankly, though I at first embraced the emergence of my own first recognizably contemporary voice with relief if not delight, that voice quickly bored me—or maybe my thoughts bored me, or my self bored me, or all of the above. Maybe I was just undergoing an early midlife crisis. The pleasures of the familiar, of anything I had mastered and could repeat, diminished. Even the pleasures of technique bored me, at least when technique functioned as an anchor to keep the mind in place rather than as a slingshot to fling me toward some spot I hadn't seen yet, just over the horizon. The urge to move beyond, to understand myself as a stranger, *estranged*, became more pressing. It got me up from my chair and moved me; I stopped waiting for my poems to arise from within as if unbidden, already spoken.

I went out looking, outside and in. I walked Jakarta and Palembang alone, navigating crumbling sidewalks and eight-lane streets streaming with constant traffic. In Paris, I found a hotel near Paris Nord, and walked to the center through working-class neighborhoods I would never have seen, past shop windows showing not designer clothes but hand mixers and old shoes mended. I walked Havana's Old Town and Malecón. The National Science Foundation sent me to Antarctica, where I walked a glacier daily, knowing it could open a crevasse beneath me at any moment. I stopped saying *someday*.

I was not trying to find myself, much less my "voice." I stopped believing I would ever know myself, or that I could even know what either term, "to know," and "myself," might mean. Can one—a mind, by which I also mean a body—ever be as whole, intact, bounded as the phrase implies?

The farther I traveled, the stranger I became.

What I wanted, what I want now, is not to avoid danger but to be a little afraid at all times –

– as I am when a storm barrels out of the north down the canyon, which concentrates the wind like a long funnel, letting it build speed and sharpen its howl. Icing over, our huge windows visibly bend and flex. I picture the moment of fracture, shards flying inward and after them stinging snow. I think of Dickinson's odd couplet, "When Winds hold Forests in their Paws/The Universe – is still – ," but not because I know what it means.

It isn't hard to be afraid, if I pay attention.

Eventually, I took joy in this.

~

Over time, I no longer knew my own work. It shed its carefulness, its overt constructedness, which I had so attentively fostered but no longer seemed to care for. I could no longer look at a page and say whether what I had put there was coherent or not, whether it was a poem or not. Fragments of experience and voice slipped around on the page, hewing close not to my idea of a poem but to the way my mind actually worked.

Was that the way my mind actually worked?

There on the page was the evidence. I wasn't sure I wanted anyone else to know. I marshalled the fragments as best I could then squirrelled them away. Eventually, I began to take them out and hold them to the light. I had stockpiled scores of them, little odd-bodied things. What, then, to make of them?

A writer who had admired my previous work asked to read them and found them remote and unrevealing. He wanted me to build the whole story, who what and where, with details, the way I used to.

My canniest friend, the one who knows me best as both writer and person, said, "They are your most intimate work."

The pressure of expectation, reputation itself, can hold a writer in place. We desire, don't we, to be known; the world desires to know us—or so we believe. I wondered, Why should it? Yet I walk into every medieval cathedral I pass, looking for art that is literally iconic, presenting images and telling stories that push my buttons every time. One flattened Madonna after another. The blood of saints, plenty of gold leaf, a lump in my throat. Imagine how startling the Renaissance was, how it deepened its depictions of reality into dizzying dimensions, and so bewildered before it blissed.

Eventually I thought I would let others decide, and started to send the poems out—mostly not to editors who knew me, who might be looking for some trace, but to strangers. Later, I gave a reading from the new poems in Canberra, to celebrate the publication of a small chapbook not coincidentally called *Bewilder*. I hadn't looked at the poems for a while, since they had been assembled. I stopped mid-reading, and blurted, to audience laughter, "These poems are very strange."

As my audience necessarily shifted, my circle of first readers narrowed from those who were looking for a specific thing they recognized, that followed certain poetic rules, to those who were happy to watch technique engaged as a catapult, to fling us all into surprise.

~

So, like a poem, this essay comes to me in pieces, as a city presents itself in neighborhoods, as the world flies at us in shards, which our trickster brains fuse together as fast as they arrive so we don't notice it is broken. Arranging. Making sense of, by which I mean subjecting to sensation in the moment, not subjecting to reason or conforming to the known world. A scrap of birdsong. A fragment of language. A firmament, singular enough to have a name, though it is made up and enlightened by billions of stars—themselves comprising atoms and sub-atomic particles in flight. I, too, remember, and you as well, that we are mostly space. If I were small enough, I could sail right through you. For all that, I am not small enough, not today. Instead, with you I ride an orb through space, and I don't even have the sense most of the time to let the ride exhilarate me.

An interruption of humming in the blood. Which brings to mind a homing –

– as if humming and homing, connected in the ear by sound, forge a more mystical relationship in meaning.

~

Meanwhile, Emily Dickinson, my perfect stranger, whom I will neither be nor know.

Meanwhile, my students, their inefficient and radiant mental calisthenics, which I am still trying to convince them are physical feats, performed by meat.

Meanwhile, the mountain lion, who knows for certain I am only meat, whose gaze held me rapt and not so much afraid as exhilarated, never so strange.

Meanwhile, we often leave the sliding door open to the deck. One summer, for no reason we could fathom, the birds that had always stayed on their side of the threshold began flying into the house. I would come home to a bird fluttering among the potted plants and along the window, trying to find *home*, to find *out*—the same.

The first one, a disoriented chickadee, I tried to urge back out the open door with a broom. Again and again, I failed—whenever I got the bird near the opening, her freedom, she veered away from it in panic. Finally, she perched, exhausted, in a rubber tree in the corner. Having reached the end of my invention, more frightened for myself than for the bird, I slowly cupped her in my hands. She sat perfectly still except for a thrumming that took her whole body. She was the size of my fist, of my heart, also thrumming. I carried her to the open door, stepped out, and opened my hands. She sat in my palm for two seconds, three, still resting. Then she opened her wings and was gone.

I have done this now a dozen times or more. To take a wild bird that way and hold it, entire, still frightens me, still thrills, still reminds me I am a stranger, even in my own house.

~

More and more, I believe in the body, maybe because I have reached an age when the bodies around me are failing.

My father, nearing ninety, loses his mind in the most material way, pieces of it, blood flow cut off, literally dying, becoming detritus, useless. The islands that still work are increasingly isolated from each other, so when he has a thought, an idea, a word, he can't connect it to anything else. Not so many years ago, he was a brilliant mathematician for whom numbers, embodied, hummed, for whom everything was connected. He was an inveterate walker; he paced off mountain ranges, his steps multiplying. Now, when I visit him in care, I wheel him to the table, and we look together at photo books of landscapes: our desert, our mountains, where he took me hiking as a child. When he comes to a picture of a place we've been together, he points and smiles. He can't say a thing, but he shows me what connects us.

In her late eighties, my mother, who has been shrinking for years, continues to erode, losing pieces of herself to the surgeon's knife, to memory, to the past. Then there is my husband, my own age, whose knees have been cut out and replaced with machines. My oldest friend had a hysterectomy; the canny one is haunted by inexplicable and excruciating numbness in her extremities. When we walk together, still for miles, she lists. We seek the city's rare flat places, because, though she can tread uphill forever, she can't get down again, so much does it hurt her feet to bear her body's force. Who knew a loss of sensation could come with so much pain?

This is just the beginning. Don't get me started.

Down time's rabbit hole.

~

I have been asked to write in this essay about creativity, a subject about which I feel inexpert at best. Instead, unsure as always what I believe in beyond the senses, I have gone gathering. What have I ever created? Nothing from whole cloth, nothing that didn't preexist itself in some other form. *Things fall apart.* Jacques Barzun tells us that Shakespeare would have goggled at us if we'd accused him of creativity. He knew it was all loot and pilfer, rearrangement, sleight of hand, the vagaries of memory and imagination, the self encountering itself in stranger form. He knew, as did everyone before Wordsworth's egotistical sublime, that only God creates.

Or if, like me, you are a nonbeliever, Nature, shuttling the same old genes into new combinations. And even Nature—after its first big invention, when anything is possible, time becomes one continuous narrowing, every moment a further limiting of options. Chances are good that I, too, will end up in a locked ward, my mind in shards, wordless. Unless we believe that choice is played out infinitely over infinite universes and our own infinite lives—in which case somewhere I am still writing long, meticulous poems about Kepler, and somewhere (perhaps even here) I sail into old age entirely intact, while somewhere else I have already died in a crevasse in Antarctica or been kidnapped in Sumatra—we are left with small beer.

Why should we be satisfied with small beer, while we still have our minds and even one universe to play in?

I spent my youth trying to become myself, by which

I mean *known*. I am still failing, happily. I have looked into the eyes of animals—so alert, so coolly curious—and been seen but not known. I have held birds in my hands, felt their entire bodies vibrating, and not known them. I still can't tell if my body is an instrument of language or the other way around. I know only that when language arises in me it becomes, with the rest of me, sinew and blood. It sings along my neurons.

Now I find no choice but to relax into the strangeness of voices, and to enter, through them, a kind of bliss.

THE POETICS OF DISTRACTION
(a defense)

> Let us strive together to part with time more reluctantly, to watch the pinions of the fleeting moment until they are dim in the distance & the new moment claims our attention.

> EMILY DICKINSON, IN A LETTER TO
> ABIAH ROOT WHEN SHE WAS SIXTEEN

I fall from a ferocious tennis family; my parents' club had both outdoor and indoor courts, and the rhythmic striking of balls on strings and concrete became a year-round soundtrack for my childhood.

Which I usually heard from the bleachers, where I sat with my book, reading being the permitted family idleness. I never managed more than three or four good shots in a row, however many balls I hit with my father or off the backboard, for which he paid me by the hour. In memory, I still hear his chant, "Keep your eye on the ball, Katharine Amanda, goddammit." I never asked why this mattered to him, and now I never will.

In ballet, I carried my arms with the best of them; my father taught me to ski at three, and I pinballed downhill among the slope's other small terrors: heedless, beside myself, fortunately never hitting another human, though I broke a few of my own bones along the way. I lost myself in swimming and eventually distance running, my body spinning my mind free. I could hit a baseball or softball almost every time, a pitch at a time, which, given my failure at tennis, drove my father crazy; as when, watching the clouds drift by from second base, I sometimes forgot to run.

At thirty, I decided to try tennis one last time. Muttering, "The ball, goddammit," I watched my soon-to-be husband's shots approach gently over the net. When my swing connected true and I didn't have to scramble for the ball, I'd fall back into reverie, perhaps composing a poem about playing tennis, badly, until I heard the *thwop* that told me it was time to turn my gaze and attend.

Real tennis players will wonder at my persistent dimness. But finally, during one of these sessions, I understood the problem in a flash: when my father admonished, "Keep your eye on the ball, Katharine Amanda," he meant not just when it was actually coming at me, on my side of the net, but, goddammit, all the time. I needed to track a flying orb from racket to racket and back, attending to nothing else, for as long as it took.

I mustered my inner obedient daughter, hit the longest volley of my life, then gave up the game for good.

~

I have been thinking about perception. When I first saw an image of what my neuroscientist friend Mark Ellisman calls the "retina of the brain," that tiny cluster of cells that receives neural impulses delivered from the eye and creates from them images of the world we believe we see, I thought, *Of course*. We've only recently learned, through the gift of scanning electron microscopes, that this site exists, but we've always sensed it. We named it millennia ago—"the third eye," "the inner eye," "the mind's eye"—imagining it provides perception beyond sight. Rather, it provides *all we know* of sight: I cherish my illusion that I see reality, the world delivered directly, unmediated, but I "see" the image I carry deep inside my skull, light projected and recreated by the eye inside my brain.

Through the retinas of my actual eyes, themselves formed from brain tissue, my brain extends itself inside-outward to perch on the windowsills of my skull. This structure and the work it does figures and manifests the fluid boundaries between what I think of as *my self* in here and *the world* out there. At this mutable border, the poem marks attention directed at once inward and outward, working to navigate liminal space, to keep everything in mind.

Some years ago, after an evening of dining in company, a friend observed to me, "You are always either completely paying attention or completely not."

I was paying attention to something else.

~

Poets may describe lyric as enacting attention arrested, focused, and distilled, but every poem both begins and ends in distraction. The poet must distract herself into attention as she writes, and the reader too performs reconstructions of the writing through a sustained distraction. The manifold poems a reader makes out of the one the poet left on the page translate the original into further diversions.

Jorie Graham's "Prayer" deeply enacts attention, if of the sort that causes Dickinson to call "labor . . . a chant" and "idleness a tune."

"Over a dock railing," Graham muses, "I watch the minnows, thousands, swirl/themselves." Leaning over her shoulder, we fall into the intense idleness of looking, as she shares her attention, so ours, between *her* looking, which *becomes ours*, and the thinking and making in which we participate, residing together in *our* eyes (inner and outer) in *her* words as they engage looking and thinking, and the consciousness, inscription, and performance of both.

We may imagine ourselves on *Graham's* dock watching *her* minnows, but seeing minnows conjured from words differs from seeing actual minnows, or photos of minnows, or minnows made, say, of paint, themselves abstractions. We bring to the poem personal docks and minnows, remembered and invented, shadowy, blurred together. We collaborate with Graham's poem in forming fleeting images, though we may not remember exactly what minnows look like. The visual centers in our brains light up like Manhattan, but the "out there" corollary for the image they manage resides in words on the page.

Already, as we see, this opening line arrests our attention in the moment it divides and places our attention in motion, quickly distracting our minds, or at least most of our minds, from the title – what was it again? – also freighted with questions: does the poem discuss prayer, enact it, meditate on what it means to be a prayer, one who prays?

Yes.

Only a one-word title, one line, and one more word in, we juggle distractions and poise ourselves for distractions yet to unfold. This is not a problem but the point. In finding our precarious balance, undergoing shifts and instabilities, undertaking to hold in mind multiple images and ideas at once, all while navigating the poem's formal enactments through syntax, line, and music, we find our pleasure, in this case created by the mind meditating, through language, on what the inner eye perceives. In traversing these spaces, it matters less how we use our senses to shuttle images or sensations from out-side, where we find our source material or inspiration, to inside, where we navigate and interpret that materi-al, than how perception and understanding occur in a mind that encompasses the entire body, and much be-yond, simultaneously – or nearly, given the 80-millisec-ond lag between what happens and our experience of it.

~

So (bear with me), it makes sense that "distract" and "distraught" have the same Latin root, "distractus," to pull apart. Poetry enacts both the very real division be-tween perception and reality, and *upset* in the sense of *disturbance*. This is good if you're looking to be not only drawn but disrupted, to throw yourself over and be be-side yourself, too, whatever might get broken along the way. Besides "abstract," another synonym for "distract" is "divert," which takes "disturb" as synonym. Also *amuse, entertain, delight,* and *enchant; interest, fascinate, absorb, engross, rivet, grip, hold the attention of* – this courtesy of every online dictionary with which I distracted myself working on this essay, thanks to the mixed blessings of Google, before diverting to Facebook to announce my findings.

I rarely go down *irrelevant* rabbit holes. In response to my ecstatic Facebook post, my friend Michael Sowder, once a lawyer, now quite a good poet and possibly a good yogi, wrote: "In law, if you are driving a delivery truck on company business and run over a pedestrian, the company has to pay. But: if you are in the company truck not doing company business but are out on a 'frolic and detour,' then the company does not have to pay. Have you considered these ramifications?"

Not least that "frolic and detour" sounds like a bee's progress as described by Emily Dickinson.

Back on Google, I found that "detour" (also the name of a company desiring to distract me with audio walking guides for my favorite cities) derives from the Old French *destor* (side road, byway; evasion, excuse) via *destorner* (to turn aside). You already remember: it too is a synonym for "divert."

~

I need at least three separate, divergent, even dissonant images, ideas, and/or facts to begin a poem, enough to create blissful anxiety through the need to manage not attention so much as the tension I generate by being myself, by traveling, reading science, and visiting labs and, for years, the studio of my long-time partner in distraction Maureen O'Hara Ure, whose paintings explode with fishes, birds, and erupting volcanoes that refer simultaneously to an outer world and an inner as detailed, specific, and abstract as that of any poem. We steal each other's words, images, and ideas, keeping each other in the corners of our eyes, beside ourselves. We never try to explain, describe, unriddle, or illustrate each other. I email poems, and I have evidence she reads them; I stand in her studio and let my eyes stray while we catch up on news and gossip and unpack the NPR story playing as I drove in. Out of coffee and wine, digression, evasion, and nearly thirty years, we've grown four installations and a couple of artists books.

~

All this, and still I must admit that distraction may produce mixed, or even bad, results. Set skiing aside: as poet Sharon Bryan says, "Walking is good for thinking,/ but not vice versa." This fall (by which I mean *autumn*), walking too fast, downhill, in dappled light, on a damaged road, I hit a pothole and got up a little bloodied and with a chipped ankle bone and a fractured wrist, though I didn't count my injuries at the time, and kept walking. Two weeks later, I went over the handlebars of my bicycle. It would enhance this essay's etymological line if my shoulder had not separated but dislocated. But art can't have everything.

A Buddhist friend said, "When writing a poem, write a poem. When riding a bicycle" – you get the idea. So I'm off again. What is a koan, if not a poem riddled, a poet if not occupied, beside herself? Walking, riding, riddling, falling, I *always* pay attention, only not always to what is in front of my feet.

~

To err means to wander, to stray; errancy means sin. Argue that a poet outside her precinct, or even inside it, "on a frolic and a detour," poses a danger to herself, and I will not gainsay you. But opening our attention to encompass not only *what* we see in the world but *how*, what it means, how it informs and shapes our minds (in which I include our bodies), and inhabiting that distraction, may bring us back. Call it awe.

The tiny mason bee, who sleeps all winter in a solitary berth, can sting but rarely does, focused as it is on frisking, plundering one flower at a time while holding the meadow in mind.

Emily Dickinson wields and withholds a mighty barb, and keeps many diversions in play, even in the smallest poem:

> To make a prairie it takes a clover and one bee,
> One clover, and a bee, –
> And revery.
> The revery alone will do,
> If bees are few.

LENS

The eye, fragile and durable, tells time, which is, in essence, a function of the brain, figuring and reconfiguring our reality. Consider the miracle that any of us can see at all, much less that we can distinguish 10 million-odd colors—but the eye is so useful it evolved independently, scores of times, in species that might as well be alien to each other, except we all came to be on a globe spinning in the light of a sun. In the human eye, the iris, the only muscle we can watch at work, regulates the amount of light that enters via the pupil, the aperture that tightens in response to brightness or aversion, eases in the presence of darkness or hallucinogens or love. My driver's license says my eyes are blue, by which it means my irises, but they can appear gray or green or any combination of the above depending on what I am wearing, the quality of light reflecting off of them, my mood. From photos and memory, I know I have my grandmother's eyes, which means not that I *see* like her but that I *look* like her.

Behind the pupil in its expansion or contraction, we find suspended the *lens crystallin*, which refracts light to be focused on the retina, which in turn creates the image the optic nerve shunts back into the brain and a cluster of cells my neurobiologist friend calls the "retina of the brain," so tiny we had to invent the scanning electron microscope to see it. When I was in high school, we could name the mind's eye, but only our intuition told us it existed.

We experience our vision in a way that makes it seem like a direct and accurate apprehension of the world. *Seeing is believing*, we say. But any face I believe I see before me is only my brain's reconstruction of light shuttling through the vision system's assembly line. Thus, science, which relies on proof, gives us so many reasons to doubt ourselves.

The lens, by the way, is metabolically active, sugar-loving though not voracious, not nearly as demanding energy-wise as the heart, say, or the brain. We also call it the *aquula*, which Wikipedia, another kind of window I open onto what may or may not be real, reminds me is Latin for "little stream." The lens is bathed and moistened by the aqueous humor in front of it and the vitreous body behind. That the eye is a tiny sea, awash, has nothing to do with our propensity to weep. Tears come from elsewhere. I have thought of the lens as stable and ongoing, but, as I should know from experience, it grows and changes shape. With age, it can develop cataracts and become progressively opaque, especially when the eye is exposed to too much bright light. Getting older, we need more and more help to see.

The lens is nerveless and bloodless. It lacks connective tissue. Depending on how you slice it, its layered laminae formed from crystallins, it can look like an onion or a honeycomb—but we don't want, do we, to rerun that particular film in the mind's eye, the razor crossing. While the rest of the eye is related materially to the brain, the lens is cousin to skin and sinus, fingernail and tooth.

Depending on what kind of animal you are and what you need to see, and through what you look for it and in what kind of light, the lens may be elliptical or spherical. Pads or fibers may focus it, or muscles move it forward and backward or tilt it in the eye, an idea that makes me dizzy. A fly's eye has many lenses, as may a mollusk's.

~

The mollusk has its own story.

~

I digress. And digress again. The world is too much with me.

~

I am considering having my own lenses replaced with new ones, human-designed and made to be as good as the old. Better, if I get bifocals. Of course, at my age my original lenses tatter and grow shabby – an eye doctor recently said they are "looking pretty ragged" – but I am thinking about replacing them before I absolutely need to, according to my insurance company, while I can still read and drive at night.

I've written the story of my eyes before, in a poem. By the age of seven, I was so myopic I saw nothing without an obscuring halo; I couldn't even see the clock, its hands glowing, at my bedside. My teacher, a kind woman, told my less-observant mother, who assumed with some reason that I simply wasn't paying attention, "I don't think she can see the blackboard." I had no idea there was anything wrong: I took what I saw, or failed to see, for granted.

Many years later, a radio producer dug up a photo that had been in the newspaper not long after: my white blond hair blowing from under a patterned silk scarf tied under my chin, blue cat-eye glasses: "a young Jackie Kennedy," the host observed to me. By the time he knew me, I was a poet, known for seeing. Back in 1968, I was marching with my parents to honor Martin Luther King after his assassination. I had insisted they bring me, though I was on crutches for a broken leg. I hated those glasses, which distorted the world by prescription, so I could see it clearly.

Occasionally, the difference between what I could see through my glasses and the blur in my peripheral vision confused my brain and sent me tumbling. By my late thirties, my nearsightedness and astigmatism could barely be corrected with any lenses. I let a surgeon pass light across my eyes, as I wrote in "Good Eye," "So I too will see by the numbers,/Cornea peeling, slice by measured slice."

The night after she had done the first eye, I woke in the small-hour darkness. "A luminous thing," I would write, "time's face/Presents itself." For the first time in more than thirty years, I could see the clock unaided.

But for weeks when I woke in the night, I continued to make my way to the bathroom with my eyes closed, "feeling my way by hand/through the familiar dark"—or with my eyes open but strangely unseeing. I had to "remind my brain to use them." "Remind," a word I used in the poem as we don't usually use it, in the material sense. There was still a neural pathway there, so seldom traveled it petered out in the weeds. *Wake, see.* I had to work to reopen it.

~

What is the difference, telling this story through the medium of prose as opposed to poetry? As a lens, what does each genre permit me to say, so to see? Prose, when it does not self-consciously deploy lyric distortion, can offer an illusion of clarity, as if we are experiencing events directly, unmediated.

Poetry, even when it arrives in sentences rather than lines, provides tools for compressing, for bending, for linguistic distortion. I hope, like a corrective lens, it lets me see clearly. It does this through figures like metaphor, which might seem to deceive, but which in this case brought me through the invisible figure that occupies "remind" to its literal origin—a use that, because poetry is duplicitous, because it is the bi- or tri-focal lens of genre, sits alongside my unthinking deployment of the word. In bringing something into memory, I return it to my mind—and am myself returned. I remember that my mind is not separate from my body, however much I feel it is; it is my body, all and only. At heart, *remembering* is material.

Here, in prose, I tease these relationships out, abstract them to make them visible and clear, hoping you won't miss any of the pleasures or annoyances I've presented. Poetry allows me to put certain kinds of pressure on the language without explanation, to count on the reader to ferret out densities. Even here, writing in prose, I want to reach for that language, and often do. But prose provides me with the space to elaborate, and the space to digress. Here, I make room for my beloved teacher, Mrs. Brothers, to appear, and now her daughter, my now-lost friend Ravonne, who, through the lens of memory, remains gawky, though perhaps she was not. I think I was not an easy child for a teacher to love—like now moody, interior, deeply day-dreamy, given neither to finishing my homework, nor to performing it as instructed. "Even now, too often,/I close my eyes to see."

Yet Mrs. Brothers saw me, and made the right diagnosis, perhaps because she saw a little of Ravonne in me. Decades later, radio producer Elaine Clark digs up my history, and Doug Fabrizio, the host, transforms an eight-year-old made self-conscious by her glasses into a figure of unconscious glamour, a fore-shadow and vision of the poet she would eventually be seen as.

After my first eye surgery, I took to calling myself a miracle of science. Having always been a distance swimmer obliged to stick to the pool, where I could follow the big black line from end to end, counting strokes so I wouldn't hit the blur of wall, I took up open-water swimming. I stood for hours at a time at my window, looking up the canyon outside, noticing distance and detail, the clarity of the hawk hovering in an updraft focusing its own hawk-eye on the smallest movement on the ground. Even now, I am fully aware of my looking, full of it; "I am living," as I say in "At Pompeii," yet another sight-obsessed poem, "on the skin of my eyes."

~

Are all my poems about seeing, or its failure? Perhaps lap swimming and its endless reversing made me a poet; maybe being able to swim in open water led me, around that time, to plunge into prose. I can't say.

When I went to Antarctica, I was given lenses to protect my eyes from too much sun. But I wanted to experience that vast space, its reflections, refractions, and mirages, all the deceptions light plays, unmediated. Not wanting those lenses between the view and me, I kept taking them off, until the sun and wind burnt my eyes.

Prose lets me tell you outright, as my vision begins to dim and blur again, that I am saving my money; I am willing to pay out of my own pocket to arrest this process.

~

In perception lies the crux of story, the crux of lyric. By perception I mean more than literal vision, but vision is a good enough place to start, a place to lose yourself, in an organ as small and complex as the eye, and a place to finish, even as we distort our vision to extend it, so we can see what grandeur lies beyond us, too small, too distant. Yes, our telescopes now as likely as not act like ears, great arrays of them turned together toward specific zones in the sky, listening; but when I hear the word "telescope" I still think of Galileo, his mind through his eyes cast upward by glass he ground himself, "levitating into the night sky," as Adrienne Rich wrote of Caroline Herschel in "Planetarium," "riding the polished lenses." I have seen, in Florence, his instruments, whose lovely wooden shapes bear his touch and so, as her envelope poems and fascicles do Dickinson, bring him forth physically, if not literally, into our time.

~

Here, now. The scientific, the personal; the literal, the metaphoric. The bodies we have and those we think we have, sailing our minds through our pasts, our visions, our words, our projections.

Literary language is full of the I, of the eye. The poem stacks up images. The story unfolds. Whatever we imagine, present or not, the visual centers of our brains catch fire.

I can feel myself becoming pedantic, saying again to my poor graduate students, trying to get them to keep more than one idea in mind at once, "Your mind isn't mystical; it's meat."

So are my eyes. And my images of iceberg, red-tailed hawk, next month's eclipse, any of you: remember that I keep them, in my mind's eye, that cluster of cells so small you can scarcely imagine it, with me.

IN THE WAY OF KNOWING

Sometimes I forget I'm a woman – at least – I
forget to think of myself as a woman.

SARAH PERRY

A young man asks the philosopher of enchantment to
explain enchantment's necessary conditions. Number
three of three is "Woman."

~

In Ubud, in rustic Balinese spa luxury, I stand swimsuited
in a shaft of sunlight before my mirror and run my clippers
nape to crown. Hair glints and falls over my shoulders.

A flash in the mirror. Five young, sarong-clad men
who have carried my bags and lit my mosquito coils,
press noses to my window. When I turn, they applaud.
I haven't caught them looking; they've caught me. Back

in the mirror, eyes on me, I resume.

~

Mary Ruefle says, "When you become invisible, you become your inner life." Not vice versa.

Dickinson says,

Are you - Nobody - too?

~

In Van Eyck's "Annunciation," Mary stands by a window, hand raised to welcome or fend off her visitor, who knows?, averting her gaze against him.

The angel bears impossible rainbow wings. The lily at Mary's feet will not fade, though she's not, depending on translation, necessarily a virgin. An old story: his desire configures her body, its power assent enough for both.

I am meant to watch.

The light's northern pallor; heavenly brocades celebrating the local cloth economy: with what optical devices, high-tech at the time, did van Eyck effect his minute brushstrokes?

Years ago, I wrote:

A machine for faith. . . .
. . . never fails

Its cue to transport. . . .
Those wings and lilies -

and they still frankly send me; the Holy Spirit, too, a dove riding a sunbeam straight into Mary's head – who looks, not coy, *absorbed*. The story teaches modesty, submission. But follow Mary's eyes. She gazes at the future, hatching her idea. Making history.

~

> I found the words to every
>   thought
> I ever had – but One –
> And that – defies me

says Dickinson.

~

D. H. Lawrence's Lou Witt says, "I am one of the eternal Virgins . . . My dealings with men have only broken my stillness and messed up my doorways."

Does archetype render us hyper-visible or invisible, machines for meaning, "pruned," à la Williams, "to a perfect economy"?

~

The philosopher disagrees with Freud on all but one *fact*: male violence is inevitable; the son *must* kill his father to marry his mother. But in the story behind Van Eyck's painting, the *father's* narrative machine kills his *son* every time, setting others to the dirty work, tick-tock. If father and son remain one, and the sunbeam-diving dove also, who gets the mother?

Both stories transport me again.

And again.

~

The spa arrays itself around the house of Walter Spies, who founded the Neka Museum for Balinese Art, dedicated to making the spirit world visible in ours.

My driver Wayan takes me to temples and sacred mountains. In my sheared head he reads devotion – Buddhist, Christian, Muslim, Animist – and takes me to a Barong dance at his home village. The battle between lion king and demon queen plays out from midnight to dawn.

Spies himself painted Bali's mythic fauna and intricate studies of actual dragonflies, butterflies, starfish.

~

A long-ago lover, an engineer, insisted long hair on women is a secondary sex characteristic. In the presence of archetype, even scientists can't always keep their facts straight.

Rapunzel, Rapunzel, let down. All that hair, but she can't climb out of the story.

The black hair on my abandoned love's head was lush as his beard. My husband's locks, pale, flow to his shoulders. Tall as a house, he flies them like a flag for me. I can spot him across any room. I may hide in the crowd, but he always knows where I am.

Can you define the other, for your own uses, without changing it?

~

In "He fumbles at your Soul," Dickinson's god doesn't plummet down a bolt of sunlight, but "fumbles," becoming plural before "they drop full | music on." The "Ethereal Blow" *about* to happen continues not to, hobbled by dashes, "further heard – /Then nearer – Then so – slow," the blow's approach alternating with retreat, sense suspended in space where waiting-in-becoming becomes its own end.

Still, Dickinson depicts divine ravishment less primly than Van Eyck, "scalp[ing]" the soul, rendering clothing irrelevant. Mind fuck pure and simple, hers is a full-body experience: mind makes body, and vice versa. In her annunciation, she takes on power in creating it, her pacing impeccable.

Female rapture comes, in her own time, through the head.

The womb has nothing to do with it.

~

Mary will never again be left unsupervised. Angels loiter. Magi drop in; beasts attend. Annunciations become an industry, and Madonnas with little-old-man-children standing on their knees.

Almost missing from the Madonna genre is Madonna del Parto, depicted gravid, though so rarely the best, Piero della Francesco's, has her own museum. "[T]his girl," Jorie Graham writes in "San Sepolcro,"

> unbuttoning
> her blue dress,
> her mantle of weather,

stripping down for the birth, desperate to have it over, *I* think, though Paisley Rekdal sees avoidance in approach:

> . . . the perspective is such
> that if I cover the painting's
> top half with a hand, Mary steps forward;
> if I cover the lower, she shrinks back,

also right. Why have we womb-worshippers so seldom painted Mary heavy, aching, afraid?   Waldemar Januszczak wonders, is "pregnancy just too real, too *biological*?" Fraught with memories, as Rekdal puts it, of times

> the mother had torn,
> . . . and no one worked
> quick enough to cut the cord wrapped
> around the baby's throat.

The child of the painting of Our Lady of Guadalupe peers from Mary's belly through a draped window the shape of an open vagina. *Biological*, with interior decoration, lit by his halo.

~

My problem is personal.

I ask the philosopher if I have a different relationship with enchantment than he, because I have a womb.

I *mean*: If your definition makes over half of us agents of enchantment available only to the other half, do you have a problem?

Yes, he says, answering, to be fair, only the part of the question I spoke aloud. He says, "Woman is the source of all life."

"Mother Earth," he says. "Gaia. It's just a fact."

~

In Van Eyck's Arnolfini portrait, the secular master, sporting a straw hat that still looks trendy today, holds a woman by the hand. Her robe is lined with tiny tufts of fur taken only from the soft chests of squirrels, thousands of them. Another lesson in economy: what happens to their bodies, their coarse and lively tails? Look over the pair's shoulders, at the mirror: you see them from behind, and facing them, the artist himself, his tunic the blue of her sleeve, a blue deeper than the window's northern sky. The man's grip tells us: he owns her dress, its fur interior, her enormous belly, the future. Everything on and in her makes her his.

~

The *New York Times* profiles Jordan Peterson, "a University of Toronto psychology professor turned YouTube philosopher," guru to disaffected young men, a few of whom express their inner chaos by gunning or running down women. He says, "Clean your rooms" (not a *terrible* idea, but) and, "Chaos [has been] represented by the feminine . . . forever," concluding, "You can't change it."

He says, "it makes sense that a witch lives in a swamp."

The reporter notes that "witches don't exist."

He, purportedly a scientist, says, "They certainly exist."

~

Like all the planets in our solar system, the Earth spun itself out of dust, made mostly of nitrogen and helium, into a planetesimal, then finally into the ground our feet so briefly tread. Looking out my window, I see leaf and branch, rock and soil. Beyond my vision rivers flow into the ocean from which all life on earth came, built from carbs and lipids, proteins and acids. Until a few years ago, we believed all life required phosphorus, but scientists have discovered a bacterium that replaces phosphorus with its toxic (to us) cousin, arsenic. There may be life forms out there, perhaps way out there, that replace carbon with silicon.

Name a planet - Mother Earth, Gaia - any way you want. Ancient Egyptians called the earth male, the sky in its distance and fire female, but naming didn't make them so.

~

A museum teeming with demons.

Another lined with Madonnas.

Walter Spies' spare and gorgeous starfish.

Dickinson, Van Eyck, my philosopher, you, I, all evolved from one single-celled organism who, around four billion years ago, probably in a swamp, split in two. Little wombless cell, little fact, thanks for your ambition. Nature worked it out: put all your eggs in one basket, you have to surveil it; you can't let it loose to roam.

Nature, on the other hand, sets little bombs everywhere and lets them explode.

Complex life may have evolved and died out many times before our higher-order ancestors arrived and eventually dreamed up witches, but for over 80% of that time the earth belonged to bacteria and archaea - and there were a lot of them. Are. Phytoplankton generate half the world's oxygen, and we who created "male" and "female" remain a tiny minority. The terms don't apply to fungi; lichens, which may live forever, reproduce asexually. Some lower plants reproduce through parthenogenesis, as do the odd scorpion, bee, velvet worm, goblin spider, pigeon and turkey; there is an entirely asexual, all-female whiptail lizard. The female kobudai fish may become male at reaching her majority; when a female attains the top of the clownfish matriarchy, the dominant male will change to female and replace her in the ranks. Scientists have recently observed a gynandromorph, a rare rose-breasted grosbeak that is rosily male on one side, golden and female on the other.

Who could resist enchantment?

~

My problem is personal *because* it's biological. Where difference exists, who is "different," and who decides what that means? As Guy Claxton says, "I am who I am because I am a body" – *this* one, female among other things, queer in its ways; to me normal, chaotic as any, no more. Every pleasure and enchantment that takes me takes this flesh.

Which has a womb. Also an appendix. Or did, though I noticed its presence no more than I do, now, its absence, and many times less, I am sure, than any man I know thinks of his penis.

Are you thinking of it now?

Most days of my life, when has my womb ever occurred to me, unless in the moment it was being inconvenient? I've thought less about reproduction than pleasure or love, which pre- and post-date my fertility. I have no children, by choice, but even most women who connect pleasure with that kind of creation will, vastly most of the time, work to prevent rather than enable it, its possibility an impediment to, not a vehicle for, enchantment. A woman's tools for doing so may make her a witch. Male imagining may constrain her.

Enchanted, I am my least gendered, most queer, beside myself, self and estranged, taken not *by* otherness but *within* it, my animal body, its desire and pleasure, its fiery orbits, its suspension and velocity in time.

Freedom, surrender.

A woman, I forget to think of myself. I forget the gaze that writes me over, Madonna or witch, and gaze beyond the frame, betraying nothing.

~

Under the microscope in the lab, diatoms, golden, arrayed with spines and tails and jewel-like structures: tiny parachutes, elaborate balloons too small to see except through miraculous lenses – no ordinary creatures; breathers-out; givers of life; ancient ones who will survive us – joining as we do into colonies fantastically shaped: stars, streamers, fans defined by bodies –

No life like this –

Beauty slips its knots, passing strange, and real.

Given a choice, taking one, I choose the sky.

Then again, earth –

Is it different for you?

FILAMENT

From late Latin *filare* "to spin," from Latin *filum* "thread."

But 'tis a single Hair –

EMILY DICKINSON

Light as air, nearly, the filament in a lightbulb is made of tungsten. Jar it, shake it, step wrong while climbing the ladder toward the chandelier – even if you don't fall or you land holding the bulb high, cradled in your palm – it might break inside for no apparent reason. Even if you see no trace of soot, if the glass ball remains perfect, you can tell the bulb is gone by shaking it gently and listening for bright music.

Tungsten is one of our hardest elements. It burns at a very high temperature, not melting even then. Inside a closed globe, deprived of oxygen, it gets hotter and hotter but won't flame. Incandescent bulbs can burn your fingers; they waste themselves.

~

Light as air, or nearly, so we think—only, most women know, hair is anything but, even when, as mine once did, it "Flits – glimmers – proves | – dissolves –" says Dickinson, glancing where the sun touches it.

Hair can hurt you if you sleep on it funny or if it dries wrong or has somehow grown a little askew. Barrettes hurt, elastics hurt, hairpins hurt, ornamented or not. Cowlicks hurt. Imagine being a sister in a famous set, performing the hair hang for one circus or another. Imagine braiding the steel cable into your hair—"Filament, filament, filament . . . Launch'd . . . out of itself," says Whitman—then allowing it to loft you above the rings and into the upper reaches of the tent while you hold your pose under hot lights, toes pointed, arms flickering.

As *The Guardian* puts it, "That's not a torture technique, that's entertainment."

You, too, would keep your weight down – 115 pounds for the heaviest Alaya sister, 90 for the lightest, so whittled, so feminine, so boyish. You would approach your spin knowing its physics: it will double your weight, the pressure on your scalp.

Which is nerve rich, exquisitely tender, as if in close communion with the brain, though apparently the brain, where we process a pain for every finest wild hair, is oddly insensate: a surgeon can cut into it without administering anesthetic, can touch the actual brain to create a sensation or a tremor elsewhere in the body, displaced. Perhaps hair acts as the brain's otherwise absent sensory system, so hurts, as it were, in the brain's place.

I know, hair doesn't hurt, itself; it hurts a direct object. Many women, I'd warrant, maybe most, have had their heads forced back by the hair, been brought to ground by pain.

My childhood friend calls her hair her "dead matter." But I imagine the brain's electricity reaching the skull, and instead of turning back on itself, extending outward, follicle by follicle. Hair raising.

~

"Tell all the truth | but tell it slant –" our lady of pure lyric instructs us. An electric animal in my brain persists in playing a game in which I try which lines of Dickinson's I can replace with lines from other of her poems similar in vocabularies, tones, and imageries. It's possible, for example, to swap out the first and third lines from "Tell All the Truth | but Tell It Slant," where the next line is "Success in Circuit Lies" with those of "To be alive, is | power," to get this:

To be alive, is | Power –

Existence – in itself –

Without a further | function –

Omnipotence – Enough –

Tell all the truth/ but tell it slant –

Success in Circuit | lies

Too bright for our/ infirm Delight

The Truth's superb | surprise

That I can do this, almost convincingly, is partly a tribute to Dickinson's deceptive formal and textural consistency, partly rooted in that wonderful word "circuit," which not only implies coming all the way around, but also invokes literal power, the flow of electrons round a closed path.

Lest I spin myself a web too tight to unknit, made possible because the poems work not by narrative, which is completely absent from them, but by substitution, I'll stop. But I could keep circling, picking the two apart and reweaving them into my lesser version – lesser not despite but because of its plausibility, because I've made the imagery consistent, and also the metaphor.

Discretion, direction. When I was younger, I might have slanted my eyes at you, glancing, oblique, sidelong; inviting or annoyed; you would not have been able to tell, unable to look right back, to close and electrify that particular circuit, unless I chose to turn and face you head on. Would you, or would you not, have understood me?

"Slant" and "circuit" contain geometric gestures, a line's infinite extension beside a circle's turn on itself, so irreconcilably different as to prohibit or annul the metaphor almost altogether.

So the metaphor in "Tell all the truth" fails, as all good metaphors must, though not all so early nor so completely. Success in difference lies, and the poem *must* begin in extremity of difference, this failure, ending as it does with movements that likewise oppose each other, however the poem insists on equating "Lightning to | the Children eas[ing]" with "Truth . . . | dazzl[ing] gradually."

If a metaphor fails too fully, it carries us into nonsense, or surrealism. But Dickinson fails with breathtaking precision. The gaps she opens don't suck us into chaos; they suspend us, spinning, agonized, exhilarated, far above the spectators, in a brilliant maelstrom, in a web of light.

I can't hold a candle to her, and why should I when I have this transparent sphere, and inside it a whisper of element heating up.

She "takes off the top of my head."

~

When I cut my hair, over thirty years ago, it wasn't, at first, quite short enough to make children stop and stare – that came later – nor yet to elicit envy from women whispering *I wish*, nor to beguile perfect strangers (teenagers, men in suits) to ask to touch my head.

Nor to cause otherwise reasonable gentlemen approaching or passing sixty, now in their cups, to cast their memories back to our school years, and lament, "How could you?" Decades later, I understand what they mourn has nothing to do with me: extinguished youth, faded potencies. Privilege, maybe; the grip they imagine they've lost, though they hold tight as ever.

My canny friend of twenty years looks at old photos and asks why. Is she sentimental for something she never saw? For lightness, for deception?

Aren't we all?

She wants only to know everything.

This is not hard to understand. Nothing could be more obvious.

~

Light: a narrow stream of gas rises from the sun in a nebula, an interstellar cloud. When my father accused me of keeping my head in the clouds, this was not what he meant, but what I felt, what I feel: lift, detachment, flame, vast distance into which all, not least myself, can vanish, and will. O joy.

Galaxy filaments are the largest cosmic structures we know, which almost certainly does not make them the largest extant. They limn the borders where two voids meet, but how do we find the place where nothing joins nothing? The numbers move us; the poem shuttles us through its lines, we hardly know how.

If the universe is a web, who wove it, according to what architecture? With eight delicate legs, with eight fingers and two thumbs, the digits we always thought to count on. In the corner of a barn, between two bushes, at a loom before the fire, with clicking needles, with her back to the wall, all day, only at night, spinning straw into gold, keeping her pattern in mind.

Penelope tore out her own work nightly and started over. So, through evasion, like Dickinson she chose her master, the absent one, who left her alone. Until he didn't.

When did I learn the spider does this, too, eats her work and spins it again out of herself, ingenious recyclist?

~

My childhood friend's braid was as thick as my bicep and golden. Unwound, her hair might have been her glory. "Dead," she would say, "excreted," gathering it into her hands, her lip curling with disgust.

~

Let's say lamp. Let's say incandescent, as my father has been betimes with rage, with joy, as he certainly was in numbers illuminating his brain, firing off its math-ematical places. On a functional MRI, my brain lights up, all of it, no matter if I'm reading a poem or turning a tetrahedron inside out and flapping it to make it fly, or awaiting instructions. The brain of my friend Fred, a mathematician like my father, works discreetly, or discretely, efficiently; on a screen, I've watched it devote one brilliant little bit of itself to the poem, an entirely different brilliant corner to manipulating geometric shapes. Otherwise, the house beneath his skull remains dark.

Later, he tells me I was supposed only to rotate and meditate on the various 3D shapes, not to open wide and animate them, unfolding and refolding them into new shapes. Who knew there were rules? The word "manipulate" means one thing to a mathematician, other things to a poet. The word "read" might also.

Let's consider my father's brain as it is now, its lamps under his still-full head of hair going off room by room, switch by switch, leaving little islands of light. If he is inside one, he can't cross to another through the space the doctor calls "white matter," by which he means dead matter, turned off. "His Boundaries—forgot—," my father can't speak of his inability to move between chambers, from one corner to another of that web; he can speak no more of anything. Unable to navigate his brain, his words can't come together with each other, with what they name. One day, in an instant, the fuse that runs his heart, his brain, will blow, and that will be that.

When he sees me, he smiles, he waves. While I sit with him, putting myself directly in his gaze, he watches me hard, listens to what I say, opens his mouth, fails to speak. "[Plying] from Nought to Nought," I wonder what, at any moment, he remembers, what room he inhabits.

Does "Himself himself | [inform]"? How can I say?

A year ago I said to him, "I wish you could tell me how you experience time," and he began to weep.

Penelope's weaving erased days. Dickinson counted nights, poem by wild poem.

My father, former mandolinist and banjo plucker, who took me to hear Pete Seeger, Arlo Guthrie, the Indigo Girls, Lyle Lovett, and the Grateful Dead, still knows he dislikes Lawrence Welk. When I wheel him into the activities room, where Champagne Music bubbles forth from the television, he musters "no," and I wheel him away again. After many trips up and down the hallways, through the cold gardens, I take him back. A minute or two later, during which he repeatedly sighs, I lean over and say, "This never was our kind of music." He cracks up.

Dickinson says, "The Love a Life can show | Below/ Is but a filament, I know."

~

"To be alive, is | power," but not necessarily freedom. Electrical power gathers and builds, it looks for a place to go, but it can travel only where drawn. It can crackle and spark; it can lift your hair to the brush, light the sky or the nerves. Trap it inside glass. It works for you.

The human body conducts electricity, impulsive, nervous, wired. It can carry a current to ground and sing.

Just thinking about it makes your hair stand up.

~

"Till the bridge you will need be form'd, till the ductile anchor hold,/Till the gossamer thread you fling catch somewhere, O my soul," says Whitman.

Years ago, I was drawn up an escalator behind a woman with the most beautiful hair I have ever seen: brown shot through with pale gold, cascading well below her waist, so thick you could have made a bed of it. I would never have dreamed of touching it, but sometimes, when I can't sleep, I imagine wrapping myself in a cocoon of hair where I hide, changing into something else. Sometimes, I dream I wake up in a hotel room, my inexplicably long hair knotted like a web. I have people to meet. I have no comb.

> A limit like the Vail
> Unto the Lady's face –
> But every Mesh – a Citadel –
> And Dragons – in the Crease –

says Dickinson. Even while admiring it, not immune to its beauty, I could see how all that hair tilted her head back, how much it must have weighed.

Not to mention the weight of the eyes watching her. I wonder if she ever cut it off.

~

Years later, a woman introduces me to an audience by assuring them I am "entirely without vanity." She quotes an interview I gave to a reporter for a church-owned newspaper who asked why I'd cut my hair. "Because," I told him, "when I account for myself, I don't want to confess I spent 10,000 hours on coiffure."

My introducer in her careful blonde do, entirely without irony, describes imagining me at the gates, St. Peter totting up hours on his clipboard.

Anyone who thinks I'm not vain hasn't been paying attention.

"To be alive – is/" *pleasure*, I might say – nobody's but my own.

~

My friend from India died at her kitchen sink. She was looking out the window into tree limbs laced with light when a vessel exploded in her head and she was discharged, no longer present or embodied. Her hair had never been cut; when she let it loose, it fell all the way to the floor.

My husband's mother died at fifty-six, of a lung cancer blown to her brain. The surgeon opened her skull and removed what he could without taking too much of *her*, shaving the hair she had kept so beautifully golden since her reign as a beauty queen. After she began chemo, the shaving didn't matter, nor the surgery. I think of her head filling and shedding, her kindhearted self, pressed out by that object, generated by her body but also foreign to it. I think of her body losing heart, filling with its own absence, and its fear.

~

My father's hair, still thick, is more steel than pepper. In my age, I would rather have my mother's, which glances and shines, pure platinum, as I once had and abandoned her polished goldenness, in my golden youth. She dyed her hair for years before succumbing to its emergent beauty.

I hope I have a brain that stays, like hers, mostly intact, though at almost sixty I already feel how the world recedes.

. I ask my canny friend, Does your hair not hurt you? Is it not a burden?

She has taken scissors to it at her bathroom sink, leaving behind enough for a handhold.

~

He hasn't spoken more than one word at a time for over a year. Today, as he's never done, my father lifts both hands toward my just-shorn skull. I bend my head into his palms, where he holds it, touching lightly.

~

It was years before I noticed the comb, still in the bottom of my travel bag – in case of what? – and removed it.

REFLECT

[T]he soul is not a soul,
Has no secret, is small, and it fits
Its hollow perfectly: its room, our moment of
attention.
That is the tune but there are no words.
The words are only speculation . . .

JOHN ASHBERY

Shadow of myself, written over, outshone, transformed. In a darkened gallery, sculptures from *The Glass System* flicker and glow, flutter and spike, my shadow everywhere, though I don't notice it until I try to take photographs and keep finding among angular shapes my head's clipped oval. Allison Leigh Holt uses glass, magnets, videos, and reflected light to "focus on consciousness as an overlooked territory that one attempts to comprehend through technologies, optics and visual models." But for once I am not thinking about consciousness, or making art, or lenses for vision and perception.

The device I still call my phone becomes in my hands a scrapbook keeping thumbed-in text, recorded audio, photos. Now, I use it to mark the range of my covetousness: I want to carry one of these cold hearths home. But which?

No smoke. Only light and mirrors.

The sculptures' outsized shadows, thrown onto the wall below, dwarf the smaller illuminated versions above. The sculptures won't show themselves without showing me, eyes gazing, abstracted.

By accident, I have begun my single photographic project, an extended doodle on reflection.

~

As 2018 turns into 2019, I become a shadow of myself. When Chris closes his good right eye and assesses what he can see of me through his left (how damaged it is we don't yet know), he describes an image circumscribed by darkness and, in the middle, growing lighter, my head, my face, rippling. He can't show me a picture of what he sees. I ask if he would know me on the street.

Once his eyesight has recovered as much as it will, doctors will go to work with lenses, which correct through refraction. Distortions or losses created by damage to the eye itself, where the detaching retina tore, and tore again, and had to be pulled and spliced, split to relieve the pressure, reattached, buckled in, mended yet again, will remain, and any more repair will be up to the brain, that remarkable organ.

He gazes toward me with his misshapen pupil and says, "I would know you anywhere."

~

Now, when I photograph objects in museums and galleries, I no longer dodge and weave, trying to get myself out of the picture. I welcome my reflection or shadow, the way I welcome charismatic birds or light on a London façade at night, as other, transitory, subject to fleeting captures.

I am everywhere, always intruding, always about to slip away: reflected in Jane Austen's polished grave marker and in the mirror set to show the ceiling of a chapel; in the sculpture garden at the Hirschhorn, where images of running children fly through mine; I walk out of a suit of armor in the window of a pricey London gallery.

I will never get closer than this.

Facebook learns to know me by reflection and files my shots both under "Your Photos," by which it means those I've taken, and "Photos of You," by which it means images of me.

~

My new sculpture, *The Glass System #2*, comprises thick square sheets of frosted glass set on end, through which video images of Allison's life flicker from below, abstracted. I can see the videos if I remove the glass sheets, held together firmly yet somehow tenuously by magnets, or if I look straight down at the tiny screen in the sculpture's base. But once their light meets my eye, filtered and refracted through the glass, they might as well be the northern lights flashing across the sky, they are that impersonal, that transporting.

I realize after I've chosen it: unlike the others my sculpture has no mirrored surfaces. It imagines only itself. I turn it on in the evening, setting it to its private cogitations in the corner of my eye as I sit under my lamp and read. When I consider it from my chair across a darkened room, my reflection, too, becomes theoretical.

~

John Ashbery puts it:

> This otherness, this
> "Not-being-us" is all there is to look at
> In the mirror, though no one can say
> How it came to be this way. A ship
> Flying unknown colors has entered the harbor.

"Self-Portrait in a Convex Mirror" takes its title and its imagery from the Parmigianino painting, "As Parmigianino did it." Its first word, "as," positions the poem: it, too, is a self-portrait; here, too, "the face . . . swim[s]/ Toward and away like the hand/Except that it [face or hand? I wonder – the answer must be *both*] is in repose." The face, revealing, "is what is," and across the line break is "Sequestered." Of course, the face, and so the hand, also become Ashbery's; the Renaissance self-portrait, which Ashbery tells us is the first of its kind, of a face painted through an intentionally distorting glass, allows him to meditate on distortion and to distort himself, "to protect/What [he] advertises."

~

In my new love for my reflection I resemble not only Ashbery but also my husband's macaw, who has adopted me, small and tufted as I am, looking more like him than any other human he knows. He loves me the way he loves his image – not out of vanity, our human misprision, but out of a desire for company. When he's feeling flockish, he perches next to his mirrored self, chortling, chortling back. He peers into toys with mirrored sides and hangs out with the bird he glimpses in the stainless steel trash can. He calls me when I come in the front door; he perches on the arm of my chair.

Under "Your Photos" are many of Merlin.

Just try to leave yourself out.

~

"[T]o protect/What [he] advertises" is so Ashbery: he never reveals, even when he confesses; he never exposes himself gratuitously, however closely he cleaves us to the contours of his mind in action. Ashbery may "set himself/With great art to copy" his image, but he understands art's distancing mechanisms as well as anyone.

What he gives us of himself is "Chiefly his reflection, of which the portrait/Is the reflection, of which the portrait/Is the reflection once removed"; that "The glass [chooses] to reflect only what he [sees]/ . . . [is] enough for his purpose."

This, of course, is the problem not only with self-portraiture, but also with ekphrasis: that "We have surprised [the artist]/At work, but no, he has surprised us/As he works." And it becomes the problem of the lyric poem, that linguistic selfie: whatever its eye falls upon turns already into something else, a reflection of self, distorted by the eye of its self-creator.

And by the eye of its viewer. As Ashbery says, "you could be fooled for a moment/Before you realize the reflection/Isn't yours."

Words, he reminds us, "are only speculation."

Ashbery's poem and the image it describes both rely, as the poem in its reflection reminds us, on the perceptual condition in which we live. We notice it only when our task requires extraordinary precision, or when distortion becomes extreme enough to startle.

The brain sees what it wishes for, at least when it can. Mine amuses me with productive misreadings, substituting a word I want to see for one that's there: "Feral Washington" for "Federal Washington," "rooftop scholar" for "rooftop solar." Nature seems to show me water in the desert, a mountain range in the middle of the ocean.

In *South*, Shackleton writes that on May 1st, he and his crew "said goodbye to the sun," on what they knew, as scientists and navigators, would be the last time for months. On May 8th at 11:00 a.m., they watched the sun half rise again, then at 11:15 set; it rose and set twice more that day, the last time, "lingeringly," at 1:20.

"These curious phenomena," Shackleton writes, "were due to refraction," intensified by cold, because of which the sun could be seen "120 miles further south than the tables gave it any right to be. The navigating officer naturally," he observes dryly, "was aggrieved."

Chris, watching a veil of darkness descending over his vision from inside his eye, knows the retina is detaching from below. I think about it, try not to think about it. Everything out there my eye turns upside down to see, my brain flips back upright, usually for my own good. It takes two images and makes them one, with depth; it corrects for my deficiencies, the fact that I am by design nearsighted in one eye and a little farsighted in the other. It shows me an image, deep in *here*, and persuades me I am seeing that very thing *out there*. To survive, I must behave as if it's so.

Ashbery writes, "your eyes proclaim/ . . . everything is surface," and that "The surface is what's there/And nothing can exist except what's there." Surface distorts: sky, water, clouds, glass. The equipment of the eye distorts, though the brain, for the most part, puts things together well enough, often, as in my case, with the aid of lenses that re-distort back to recognition.

My husband already has an artificial lens in his damaged eye, replaced years ago by the same cataract surgeon who will excavate the damage after the retinal specialist is finished. He tells us he can now reshape the artificial lens *in situ*, the way my natural lenses have been reshaped with lasers.

He says, "We haven't done many in humans yet. But there's a bunch of bunnies in the basement who can see really well."

Really? How do you know?

~

Time, which tells the crew of the *Endurance* when they should feel entitled to succumb to darkness, distorts: light takes time to travel from the eye to the convex mirror's surface and back again, through the eye, into the brain, which constructs not only an image but an idea of the image. Parmigianino takes time to paint the portrait. The painting waits centuries for Ashbery's reflecting eye and mind to meet it; Ashbery takes his time, surely, to write his sprawling poem. French for "weather," Ashbery reminds us, is "Le temps, the word for time."

Can we then even say "what yesterday/Was like," beyond "a peculiar slant of memory?" Time was I thought I knew "Self Portrait" well; I wrote about it in school in the '80s and again in 2000 for a lecture I gave in Saarbrucken, where I could not for love or money persuade German university students, those persistent Romantics, to like it. I can't retrieve either essay, I wrote them so many computers ago. Now my attention turns to moments I don't recall as important from those early reflections. Still, as Ashbery says, "Mere forgetfulness cannot remove it," and I feel old affection returning, as if this poem could be the same one I loved then, and again, and can't remember.

The meditation on time and memory into which the painting launches the poet collapses image and material, "So the room [of the painting, of the poem] contains [its] flow like an hourglass," the "flow" of the sands from which glass is made, "hissing/As they approach the beginning of the big slide/Into what happened." No more can the poet resist turning sand to glass and so "the painter's/Reflected face" as we "[look] through the wrong end/Of the telescope." The lens here encompasses both hourglass and the curved surface of the mirror through which the face of the painter reaches us in time. So, as we've already seen, "this past/Is now here," arriving via a funhouse mirror-hall, in which, Ashbery says, "the whole of me/Is seen to be supplanted" again and again and still "always," like a wave of flowing sand, "cresting into one's present."

Thus, "the soul/Establishes itself."

The condition of looking.

"Those assholes/Who would confuse everything with their mirror games," Ashbery also says, "Are beside the point."

Including him, of course.

Including me.

HOW ARE YOU FEELING

[W]hen I try to organize - my little Force
explodes -

EMILY DICKINSON

. . . oh, yes, yes, the matter goes on,

turning into this and that, never the same thing
twice: but what about the spirit . . .

A.R. AMMONS

This morning, when I opened my mouth to answer Chris,
nothing came out.

How am I feeling?

Contagious? Dying?

I feel fine. Only, I can't tell you.

~

Don't blame my laryngitis. I can't compose myself. Assembled on the fly, disintegrating, my body/mind rework each other in time, haphazard, simultaneous, feeling/not feeling: beside themselves, "in uncertainties, mysteries, doubts."

Notwithstanding that cold fish Wordsworth, a poem isn't emotion. It's words.

~

Do you know "feeling" when you feel it or when you compose it? A.R. Ammons says his poems arise in response to,

> a more or less recurrent anxiety . . . under the
> stress of [which he] look[s] for. . . . a configuration outside as in nature . . . that seems to have
> in it the capability of meeting *the feeling* [that]
> seems to be released onto what one sees . . .

"A distraction," the poem begins, not in woe, or joy, but in pressure.

Poet as overinflated tire.

Pssssssss.

~

My husband, Chris, a visualization scientist, alive in neural space between his eyes and brain, knows how to fix things. In extremity, he seeks something to repair, a "marvelous distraction."

Between what he knows and what he can fix:

His adored mother, dead at fifty-six of brain cancer – so he builds visualization tools to help surgeons locate and remove tumors and aneurisms;

His vision, faltering twenty-five years later – already expert in seeing, he makes himself an expert in the retina;

The macaw he named Merlin at seventeen, alongside whom he lived for 42 years, who faltered and died over the course of a single day – he orders an autopsy, to learn what he should have done.

Since when is knowledge power?

Every body he's ever loved. Mine, his: too late.

~

Dickinson writes,

> After great pain, a formal
> feeling Comes –
> The Nerves sit ceremonious,
> like Tombs –
> The stiff Heart questions, 'was
> it He, that bore,'
>
> And 'Yesterday, or Centuries before'?
>
> The Feet, mechanical, go round –
> Of Ground, or Air, or Ought,
> A Wooden way. . . .

Abstraction under pressure in search of structure, this one radical, its feet – hers, the poem's – all embodied.

Likewise, "I felt a Cleaving in | my Mind —/As if my Brain had | split" names "mind" and "brain" as separate. Doing so, it identifies a full-body feeling other than (or one with?) the organ in our skulls. The poem refuses to distinguish sensation, emotion, thought.

A broken heart, a missed beat, a fracture in time: not everything is subject to fixing.

I take her at her word.

~

Skyping in, I called, "Where's my birdie?" Merlin ran to the screen to dance, chortling madly, looking behind for my entire self, making a call pitched only for me: where was I, where was my smell?

Being given a name by a bird made me – someone else.

He just got old. His heart failed, as will ours. We buried him under primroses, in a box satin-lined to cradle a fancy fifth of whisky. We kept his longest tail feathers, so he fit.

Out of grief, disproportionate, we measure graves and bury ourselves.

To rise again, some of us make poems, which arrive as feeling's measure and occasion.

~

If "the chameleon poet . . . does no harm from its relish of the dark side . . . any more than from its taste for the bright [because] both end in speculation," as they also begin, emotion is incidental until made present. If we believe "not one word [Keats] ever utter[s] can be taken for granted as an opinion growing out of [his] identical Nature," how can his poem arise from feeling?

Nursing his brother, Keats rehearsed his own dying. He didn't make poems because he grieved, no more than Chris does visualizations. Because he grieved, as we can see in the gap between the early poems and late, he made himself a poet.

The odes enact an effort toward oneness, arising from anxiety, "irritable reaching," and ending in evacuation, a release of thought into structure, then through and from it, into feeling.

"Nightingale" begins in numbness and ends in disorientation.

"Melancholy" begins in admonition – "No, no" – then advises,

> But when the melancholy fit shall fall
> > Sudden from heaven like a weeping cloud,
> That fosters the droop-headed flowers all,
> > And hides the green hill in an April shroud;
> Then glut thy sorrow on a morning rose,
> > Or on the rainbow of the salt sand-wave,
> > Or on the wealth of globed peonies . . .

– "on a morning rose"?

Pssssss. *Don't* indulge drear analogues; go to the "rainbow of the salt sand-wave," the "wealth of globed peonies" – lovely "configuration[s] outside as in nature," in which feeling *not* named takes shape. The poem's effectiveness arises precisely out of tension created by the gap between feeling named and enacted, between internal stress and external form. In the rose he finds a structure and complicates sorrow, constructing it in and through pleasure, dark and lovely, complex, as if emerging from the poem's form.

If "nothing startles . . . beyond the moment," the moment startles. Keats continues, "[I]f a Sparrow come before my Window, I take part in its existence," seeking feeling and finding it in identification, re-embodiment, projection.

~

If the brain as an organ is nerveless, from sense the mind recomposes itself, writing over what the body knows.

Chris's eye surgeries and their failures, ongoing, return in us a lifetime of loss: parents, siblings, friends, beloved animals who never will return – "Longing, we say," Robert Hass reminds us, "because desire is full of endless distances."

There have been famously blind poets, as well as sick ones. Why not? Poetry inhabits the whole body.

The world is lovely. Look hard. Close your eyes.

~

For release, I run, because I have made myself a runner. Or, idle, I check email, Facebook, though such devices don't transform anxiety; they crank it up. A poem may be a machine, but not the reverse. A machine that's not a poem diverts you from emotion; a poem delivers you to it, it to you.

The failure of artificial intelligence is, Ben Marcus says, that a computer can't distinguish me from my reflection. To a computer, a word means one thing at a time. Human language, strangely mutant, becomes a vehicle for projection. My poem says I am an "ice/-hearted bitch," which I don't feel until I write it, then I do, so I am.

Cold or hot, as his title implies, in "Fire and Ice" Frost writes not out of desire nor hate, which he names, but out of internal pressure, into a structured opposition, in which "for destruction ice/Is also great/And would suffice."

Cold eyed, colder hearted, coldly present to its demands: you don't make a poem while weeping. Compose yourself. The poem composes in itself, in the poet, and in the reader a feeling that lies unknown until encountered and uniquely named.

Then, *mind the gap*. The poet's done, gone, abandoned, beside herself, unmade.

Just in time.

BLIND SPOT

I underestimate the power of my connection with other people, with animals and events that are coincident.

MEI-MEI BERSSENBRUGGE

Sailing a strew of stars, we wonder what the dark is made of: absence or presence, nothing's strange weight.

Forty-five years ago, my school friends and I would drive on summer nights into the foothills where I now live, work, relentlessly walk. We'd sit on the wall that marked the upper border of the Salt Lake City Cemetery, once the edge of town. Below the graveyard's sweep into blackness, the lights of downtown glimmered, the city's main thoroughfares streaming south through the dark toward Sugarhouse, gathering into pools of light at South Salt Lake, Murray, Holladay: an illuminated outline of geographies we knew. Looking up, on a moonless night we could see the Milky Way.

Now, lights brim the valley floor, almost a thousand square miles. Dangling my legs from the same wall, I can still trace major arteries, densely surging with cars; I can guess at the location of Sugarhouse, where my canniest friend now lives, but I can no longer discern the absence that defines the light, negative space where bodies nestle invisibly, keeping secret.

A half-mile above me, overlooking a canyon too steep to build, my house marks the exact line where the city's sizzling wires end.

~

To cross the edge of knowing, humans fashion lenses. Leuwenhoek and Hooke invented microscopes to see deep inside what had been seen before. I've stood before Galileo's telescope, bearing the mark of his hand, the telescope which – the 16th century being that dark – he rode from a Tuscan hilltop into the unknown. The ear now included among "far-seeing" organs, in Hat Creek you can visit the Allen Telescope Array, a hectare of dishes cocked to eavesdrop on the universe when we're not looking, requiring the absence of noise, not of light, to work.

We strain to understand, to "[look] while realizing," Mei-mei Berssenbrugge writes. "In the shadow of a hummingbird . . . the energy of a moth," we replace an old idea with one we've imagined but haven't apprehended yet –

    – a glimmer we scribble on the back of a napkin in numbers, or dream –

    – but don't yet mind.

~

This morning, the *New York Times* reports the death of Iman, Malaysia's last Sumatran rhino. Singular, she bore a human name.

Almost a hundred years ago in Borneo, native loggers drew a map of the jungle in the dirt with sticks, tracing animal trails, rivers, ravines, while my grandfather sat on his heels and imagined that terrain into being. Doing so, he began its ruin. His journal reports that, in 1929, Sumatran elephants, now also all but vanished, routinely ravaged his jungle camps. Adventurer, surveyor, renowned stalker of geographies, he prospected for oil to fuel us at a time when oil seemed endless and the skies absorbed all the smoke we could make.

I, too, can walk all day, pacing pavement, mostly, human wildernesses blazing through the night. With loggers, trophy hunters, others like himself working to make the earth yield, even now he sets me moving, on wheels or burning over oceans and continents on wings.

Through telescope or microscope; the compass, the chart: "I see," I say to you, acknowledging vision's territorial claims on understanding, how it seems to cast us out into the world.

~

Decades ago, when we moved onto the knife-edge of wilderness, my husband, Chris, installed automatic outdoor lights, forestalling Dickinson's

> larger – Darknesses –
> Those Evenings of the Brain –
> When not a Moon disclose a sign –
> Or Star – come out– within –

and forgetting we can, as the poem says, "grow accustomed to the dark."

> When they saw us move, the lights came on
> and the sky vanished.

~

One fall night, I heard an owl call, another answer from the Gambel oaks below the house. Chris hammered a nest box in the maple next to the walk. At dusk, the male flew and returned, as our motion-triggered camera showed us, with worms, mice, one unfortunate vole. He also triggered the light, owl-eyes, reflected in the pictures, startling to vivid blindness.

Just as Chris, vision failing, wants light, we put it away.

~

Mei-mei writes, "A space opens and awareness gathers it in."

Through his nearly blinded eye, Chris claims to know the space I occupy. Even fully-sighted, he could never find the yogurt. Now I rearrange refrigerator shelves: his tofu and egg salad sit precisely where he will see them when the light comes on; his milk and flax seed in the door, elbow-level. For reading, he rigs up a wall screen that mirrors his computer, magnified so his eye and brain can work around the space where words vanish.

This is real. It's all in his head. What do we take literally?

Science seeks accuracy. Misses. Corrects itself.

Yet, like Dickinson, we "fit our vision to the Dark - / And meet the Road - erect," more or less.

~

Like, unlike: the owl wings into our world on the genetic remains of dinosaurs, most gone extinct when asteroids hit the earth an eon or so ago, wiping out creatures who understood it as it was then. The oil I burn didn't arise from the bodies of dinosaurs pressed and transformed by the earth for my use, though a picture book told my child self it did. The oil began millions of years earlier, when tiny plankton, not charismatic enough for a story, not thinking about the future much less me, died and drifted to the bottom of the sea.

Owls lost their daytime vision to see through the dark.

Our indoor dinosaur, Henri, lives in the light. A young Senegal parrot, still growing into his head, he tucks in his beak at sunset and whistles for us at dawn. We've just learned his warning call: two sharp quick notes struck at the sight of the meter reader or a red-tailed hawk hovering over the canyon. He watches our feeder for the chickadee, Forbush's "bird masterpiece beyond all praise," who can in her own words tell other chickadees, the bilingual squirrels, even us if we listen, where she is and whether a nearby raptor is large or small, quick or dull, on the branch or on the wing.

Surely dinosaurs conversed.

Poetry's fundamental figure, metaphor, opportunistic and changeable as DNA, roots itself in error and the grubbiness of language, relying less on likeness than on the gap failure opens.

Chris's brain works to rewire itself, to fill in blanks in his foveal vision, at the very center, where his retinal cones have stopped receiving signals, or stopped transmitting them, or both.

The sky illuminates Dickinson's "Evenings of the Brain -." My brain, all I know of the universe, is not the universe writ large, though it may or may not be "evening" in any sense of that word. My mind, busily observant, collapses then reopens the space between things that are like and unlike, or only sound alike, to understand time, erasure, agency, too-muchness: something I thought I knew.

Mei-mei says, "Estimation supports the magic of deepening."

As does precision.

~

Astronomer Mordecai-Mark MacLow's slide show on "The Birth and Death of Stars" lands in my Cloud box as I prepare for a program with him and Mei-mei on *Poetry, Deep Time, & the Stars*. Given his sparse notes, meant for himself alone, I succumb to beauty, and think, *the eagle nebula is not an eagle.*

Also: centuries before the Hubble saw this, Herschel appropriated the word, *nebula*, from Latin, *mist, vapor, cloud*. Which nebulae, mostly a powerful lot of nothing, look like from an un-lensed distance, and are not.

NASA's web page says the Hubble "observ[ed]" the nebula, as if the fly-by machine might note significance, or make a comment.

"Once there were no stars," Mordecai's notes remind me. And that astronomers named that time "the Dark Ages," after a human darkness, a not-seeing, timeless.

Nebula can also refer to "a clouded spot on the cornea causing defective vision," neither seen nor seen through.

Even our canyon, stretching north into mountains, lies under light-smudged sky. This late autumn night, few stars shine weakly through, a human city rendering the universe abstract.

~

But not absent. Maybe, as mathematician John Burgess said to Errol Morris, "the stars can't be socially constructed."

Only in us. Once – begging Mordecai's forgiveness – we were all astronomers, scanning stars for news about seasons, time, where we live, even about our futures, though we gaze into the past, the light from each star a trace of history, arriving.

In real time, if you don't blink, the death of a star could terrify.

In the not socially-constructed sense, stars aren't born, don't die, but even physicists apply biological language to their emergences and vanishings, bemoaning an event so grand we assign it precious, puny human weight.

~

Mind, a poem constellates around dark matter. Reading, I attend to words flashing by and also to what I can't see, nature and history pressing invisibly, freighted.

Let's be clear: erasing Dickinson, who simultaneously erases *herself* and proliferates, can't improve but only reads her, while perhaps also amusing. A vandalism like

> "Hope" is the thing with feathers –
> That perches in the soul –
> And sings the tune without the words
> And never – stops at all –

raises from dark matter questions about syntax. Does the erasure say "'hope' feathers the soul" or "the soul stops all"? Where does the poem find *its* soul? Does it matter?

Better to erase a glossary of ice, Ayn Rand, NASA's web page, me.

~

Considering distance, measure time. If Boise is forty minutes by air – four and a half or five hours by car, depending who's driving – how many miles? If I check, I'll forget again. Maybe 18,000 heartbeats: on that dark highway I see only what my overdriven headlights show me, mile markers too quickly flashing by.

Mordecai notes, "This precisely determined redshift indicates that the red rest-frame optical colour arises from a dominant stellar component that formed about 250 million years after the Big Bang, corresponding to a redshift of about 15."

Or,

This precisely determined red**shift** indicates that the red rest-**frame** optical colour **arises** from a dominant stellar component that **form**ed about 250 million **years after** the Big Bang, corresponding to a redshift of about 15.

"Space is a psychological property," Mei-mei reminds me.

My canny friend says, "The absence of stars is an illusion."

And their presence.

~

Likeness, failure. In our friends' rooms, conversation whirls around the fate of the earth's vanishing creatures, at least those we love.

As if this is new.

I read in the morning *Times* about a comet visiting our galaxy from another, only the second ever observed. I wouldn't now, from under my bubble of light, see an asteroid coming, though it comes nonetheless. I have even more trouble imagining *myself* as an asteroid.

So much for the naked eye. What I can't see sends me.

My grandfather was nicknamed Brutus, a word that died with Latin but endured in "brute," meaning "savagely violent." He called the elephants *rogue*, also meaning "savage," already raging.

~

Claiming, the night gone rogue, to be "Done with the Compass – /Done with the Chart," Dickinson embarks directionless on the void, making reverie a lens and human vision fallible.

Science, too, inches back the boundaries of imagination. Mordecai's work reminds us: time exists on scales so vast we can't apprehend them. Attending to nature, trying to bring even stars in close, Mei-mei recalls to us what we stand to lose.

If I can't escape this, good riddance?

In about 7.6 billion years, the sun will swallow whoever remains, not still including screech owl or elephant, any human, the forest of native oak below my house. In geologic time, unmanageable, animal species that have survived erasure by light, smoke, our every catastrophe, will have become new species, probably small and quick at first, possibly winged, likely overflowing with conversation. So birds made themselves once out of a ruined world, and Henri, flirting, shaking his tail, rides to breakfast on my hand.

Earth, in a universe that becomes visible once more from here, will persist in the absence of Iman, of that vole, all we evolved to love –"the blight man was born for" – and, a cauldron, will boil up life again.

~

"A vein of experience contiguous with another is called the effect of time, a separation," Mei-mei says.

And, about the uncharismatic mosquito, "one's tie to an insect is an imaginative truth." Whoever fills the space my familiars vacate may be lovable, lovely, to whoever stands in for me.

The world I construct from observation and memory and carry inside me dies when I do. I mourn my vanishing familiars while I may. I won't see to know any other earth, once I scatter in atoms, selfless, uncreatured, neither glad nor not glad.

Who will betray? Who be cast out?

Why let deep time hypnotize me, the light from stars long gone? Earth doesn't need me to walk its paths, read poems, mourn; nor my grandfather to revive him. The world my eyes and memory build inside me dies with me; still, the Milky Way exists.

I seek what Mei-mei calls "a saturation of feeling in cyclical time." For now.

Invisible to ourselves, we see farther than our predecessors would ever have believed, to the beginning, and so the end.

When Henri spreads his green wing to show me its design, he means *look*.

Mine eyes dazzle.

MY OBJECTS OF AFFECTION

Death sets a Thing significant

EMILY DICKINSON

1.

My father died in my hands, or under them, laid on; also under the hands of my mother and brothers and nieces crowding his bed for his last slow breath. When I first heard his death rattle, three days earlier, I knew what it was from Victorian novels, a sound I will no longer have to conjure for myself out of words on a page.

During the days he took to finish, we moved in and out of his room, going home to sleep and shower, bringing back his favorite carry-out to pair with wines he would have loved if he hadn't been too preoccupied to drink them. We told stories around his bed, not holding him here but weaving him, the man we had once known, back into time.

Then – so suddenly, after the waiting – the seconds between his breaths extended, until finally he stopped laboring and became palpably, by which I mean *to touch*, not a self but a body. It was late February 2020. None of us had any idea what he would save himself – and us – by dying when he did, in a memory care unit that would be closed to visitors within weeks. While his body cooled, we milled around his bedside, unraveling tight-knit awe into loose ends: hunger, boredom, a rising anxiety to move back into our lives –

– not yet, and never the same. To be doing anything, we gathered the room's possessions: photos, books, banjo, flannel shirts, mathematical proofs my brother had taped to his door in lieu of the usual decorative wreath or plaque, all of it no longer his.

Our arms laden, at last we left his body, past all that, to be transported to the medical school for its last use.

~

As the pandemic rolled over us and we shut ourselves in, the English poet Paul Munden, known also for giving others interesting things to do, tagged me on Facebook. For his "From Our Confinement" invitation, he asked ten friends, one a day for ten days, first to post images of the spaces in which we'd sequestered ourselves, and second to tag one friend a day of our own to do the same.

The question: Where are you?

Which came to mean, With what?

Books on books.

Musical instruments lying silent on shelves or leaning against chairs, waiting to be plucked, blown, tickled.

An antique spindle. Carved and painted masks; artifacts of obscure origin and meaning.

Andy in Winchester, Jen and Shane in Canberra, Alvin in Singapore, Jesse Lee in Uruguay – here in Salt Lake City Lisa posted carnival-bright folk art and Susan whimsical ceramic birds. Around the globe, writers and artists looked over rooms for compositions to set a mood and say – what? – about them, hiding their artful messes and delivering tight shots of corners and halls, doorways moodily lit.

From me, a sea fan, a sculpture of glass and light, a small bronze statue of an ordinary man. My grandfather's ebony elephants with their tiny ivory tusks, acquired a century ago on the other side of the world. Arrayed across the top of my bookcases: my father's mandolin, lute, Spanish bandurria, keeping their songs to themselves. Things I have to look at in place and time, filling me with longing –

– remembering the dead, whose rings I wear on my fingers, their brooches pinning my throat. Recalling me to the world as it still is, out of reach. I cancelled trips to London and Paris, to Sydney, New York, Boston, San Antonio. When will any of us go so far again?

Along with objects, my own photos backgrounded by windows, which, my house being a glass shoebox, I could only use:

—here, at dawn, a snowy canyon emerging into view outside, and, reflected from the inside, a lit-up kitchen. In between, my barely discernable reflection—

—a day later: my treadmill in its welter of cords, beyond which the same canyon greens suddenly out of snow into spring—

—all day, my rooms filling with clouds and birds, deer, the occasional fox—

—becoming an inner life.

~

I willed my Keepsakes - Signed away
What portion of me be
Assignable - and then it was
There interposed a fly -

With Blue - Uncertain - Stumbling Buzz
Between the light - and me -

Dickinson's "I heard a Fly buzz" opens with a rattle, vibrating the whole sensory self. Inside "the Room" and outside, it makes itself felt as presence "Between the

Heaves of Storm," the threshold from which the "I" of the poem speaks.

Not the threshold but the windowsill, where at poem's end the fly will simultaneously emerge into visibility and erase vision, along with hearing, all sense. In the poem's extended metaphor, Dickinson uses this confusion of sense, and its obliteration, to think through the passage the body undertakes to become, like all things, subject to possession.

"I willed my keepsakes," she says, "Signed away/ What portion of me be/ . . . ." Suspended in the line break between "be" and "Assignable," she elides the question of what "Assignable" objects may be left by will, suggesting instead that she is "sign[ing] away" what of *her* will remain here after death. Yet the body, as a rule, occupies a different category than "Keepsakes" – except maybe in its nonperishable bits, a lock of hair braided or the bleached finger bone of a saint; or unless, like my father, this speaker donates herself to science, to be parsed and weighed, studied and quizzed. As the body is at last dismantled and returned, its speaker's earthly "Keepsakes," in their passage from her possession to the possession of others, in time become not only all that can be kept of her, but at last all there is, the only "portion of [her]" that anymore "may be."

After that line break on "be," which places us into paradox, the poem falters in its strict rhythm, first forcing by means of the insistent iamb a hard stress from the last syllable of "Assignable," which in ordinary speech wants to be half-swallowed. Here, it can't be, since it's followed by the marked hesitation of " – and," which cannot bear weight so at once forces the stress backward to "ble" and shifts us emphatically along to the "then" that follows.

Thus, the act of assignment itself brings on the poem's anticipated end and closes its temporal circle: "And *then* it was" (my italics) – the precise moment in which presence becomes past – "There interposed a fly." In re-introducing from the beginning the "Blue – Uncertain – Stumbling Buzz" it seems also to enact, the line marks the final turn of the poem, where hearing gives way to sight. Between them, the windows and the eyes create the space in which the fly's "interpos[ition]" occurs. If before the fly existed sonically both inside and outside the body, now it comes visually "Between the light and *me*," "me" being the self as a whole and not merely its eyes, which the poem is careful not to name here; where the poem does name the eyes, back at the beginning of stanza two, they appear not as instruments of the speaker's vision, but as outlets "wrung dry" of the grief of others.

If a window can't "fail" in the way a body can, the fly interferes with the light at the whole site of presence. In its final line, "I could not see to see," the poem through repetition substitutes understanding for physical vision, distinguishing them in the moment of their mutual failure. I take this action of vision and its failure literally, *physiologically*. As the eye communicates back into the brain, so brain reaches itself outward into the eyes, the connection between the two intimate and material. We look not at or through but *with* our visual apparatus, however unpalpable, even speculative, our nervous systems make our looking – by which I mean that unless something goes wrong, the eyes in their seeing feel like nothing, enabling presence without our noticing them. But acting as the transparent boundary between interior self and the world out there, they are anything but nothing.

~

As Dickinson asks elsewhere, or everywhere, "Go we anywhere/Creation after this?"

The magic of the artifact, the thing once touched by, once made by, even once part of the body of the other. You can see this poem *in her own hand*, as we say, by which I mean online, where I often visit it. The first time my Googling landed me on the Emily Dickinson Archive, a joint project of various holders of the original manuscripts, and called up the handwritten version of "Long years | apart – can | make no | breach ," my body fizzed. Likewise when I opened *The Gorgeous Nothings*, the coffee-table-sized edition of Dickinson's envelope poems in, yes, gorgeous facsimile. My students, when they encounter the poems, talk about how the handwriting, enacting a mind not regularized in a print medium that couldn't accommodate them, at once frustrates them and gives them a palpable sense of freedom. Still, none of this compares to being present with the actual pieces of paper, on which Dickinson's own hand penciled words still in motion on pages I once leaned over a glass case to decipher.

She was writing for the future. The pencils lived in her pockets, nestled with scraps of paper she would write on, had written on, would reach her hand in to find. She wore those fragments. They had walked through the day with her, secreted in her famous, misunderstood white dress.

2.

My California friend, whom I believe I see quite clearly in my mind in both her younger and her fairly recent selves, claims to have the capacity neither to store visual memories nor to make images in her mind. Of course, when I finally see her again, though she will not look exactly as I picture her, I will know her. And I must ask her: how does she recognize me every year (but not this terrible year, or next) across a huge conference center or on a crowded street, if she doesn't keep an image in her mind?

Technically, you might say she has no capacity to *imagine*, but my friend writes vivid and musical narrative prose in which characters and objects come alive in their surroundings, which also come alive. I remember powerfully across thirty years a character in one of her short stories emerging into an unexpected sexual flush, can still see the blushing, almost overripe loosening of her body, that object, as desire hardened. From an essay my friend sent me just this spring, I carry an image of a river, an inner tube, an adolescent girl riding downstream past a man on shore, who, as she drifts by, manhandles his own eye-riveting thing, willing us all to see it. People, objects, landscape: whatever my friend did or did not visualize in her own head as she wrote – nothing, she claims – she doesn't *need* to see them. She has only to name them to lock me into a narrative stream.

~

In a fit of abstraction, Anne Carson says, "When the mind reaches out to know, the space of desire opens and a necessary fiction transpires."

Of an apple left high in an otherwise bare tree in Longus's novel *Daphnis and Chloe*, she writes, "The apple flies while standing still."

Flies *away*, I think, seeing that apple, apple-red in my mind's eye, though this is not what Carson says. The actual distance between me and the apple remains the same, but it seems to increase with desire.

Carson's translation of Sappho's fragment 105A goes,

> as the sweetapple reddens on the high branch
>   high on the highest branch and the
>   applepickers forgot—
> no, not forgot; were unable to reach.

The apple I see remains unfixed and mutable, personal and idiosyncratic. Different from all others, maybe only mine escapes.

~

More poets than we may think are sparing in their imagery, or at least its elaboration – Dickinson, too, for whom "'Hope' is *the thing* with feathers" (my emphasis). I don't get to see the world lying outside Dickinson's failing windows, whether there might be an apple tree with a single unpicked apple, or on how high a branch it flies, overtaking what feathered thing. Nor does she show me the keepsakes inhabiting her poem's room's interior, though I may bring to mind an image of Dickinson's actual room, where her pockets hang in Amherst for pilgrims to visit. Even her fly brings not its visible self but all-encompassing darkness, the field of vision narrowing inside the room and the singular body, while "the space of desire" and the "necessary fiction" that arises from it, are foreclosed.

Not that Dickinson eschews imagery when she needs it – think of that "narrow fellow," whose "zero at the bone" effect depends entirely on our seeing, riveted, "the Grass divid[ing] as with a Comb" – but any constructed presence, when it's there, relies on the rhetoric and requirements of the poem.

In an expediency of naming, for example, "To make a prairie," to which I can't help returning, composes its brief self, a kind of instruction manual, like this:

> To make a prairie it takes
> A clover and one bee, –
> One clover and a bee,
> And revery.
> The revery alone will do
> If bees are few.

Of this, an imagination (the poem's deceptively colloquial "it," inhabited perhaps by a god but certainly by the poet, who is the real power here) begins by creating, in mind, the first line's entire prairie, then (Focusing down? Scaling back? Reversing time?) removes that prairie, leaving merely "a clover and one bee," one of each, no more. How careful she is with her articles, and how playful. The reversal – "one clover and a bee" – becomes, subtly, not repetition but substitution, which asks us to linger on difference in sameness. As with metaphor, the substitution of one thing for another not-quite-the-same thing opens up space in the poem, refusing to move the reader forward, instead sending her back, then forth, then back yet again, to consider the poem's distinctions and what they might mean.

There's not a single descriptor in the poem. If you see a clover and bee, you've let their names drag pictures with them (or not, in the case of my friend), which your own visual cortex supplies, lighting up exactly as if the objects have presented themselves before your eyes. What the poem itself offers is not imagery but a conceptual act, a movement of the mind.

Meanwhile, the distance between "one clover and a bee" on the one hand and "a prairie" on the other blows open Anne Carson's "space of desire" for me to inhabit, and you, dizzy and in motion, as does the distance between the reaching hand and the apple, which we fill with our selves. The poem becomes ". . . the action of reaching out toward a meaning not yet known," and not to be known.

"Like a face crossing a mirror at the back of the room, Eros moves," Anne Carson tells us. "You reach. Eros is gone."

Knowledge, like meaning, is hardly the point. If the poem means to tell me how "to make a prairie," the instructions couldn't be simpler. But Dickinson, a serious botanist, would have known they could never succeed, whether to make *your* prairie you're counting on propagation through seed, in which case you need at least two clovers, or through root spread, in which case the bee is superfluous.

Either way, "it takes" near enough forever.

~

When I think of my father these days, I almost always picture him outside, often eating – sitting on a restaurant patio or the long veranda of my now-sold childhood home, or high in the Wind River range, perched on a rock beside a glacier-fed lake with a chunk of hard salami in one hand and a pocket knife in the other. In a minute, he will use the tip of the knife to winkle a smoked oyster from among its fellows, bedded in their rectangular tin; before long, he will toss me an orange, and I will fail to catch it, since as usual I'll be paying attention not to the fruit that flies toward me but to the one that escapes. I can see all of this: light glinting on the water, the wind in the trees, a cloud shredding its weather over high peaks. My father, I am sure, can see trout glimmering just under the lake's surface; equations hum in his head the way sentences hum in mine, different grammars rearranging the world's furniture, making order or its opposite. I smell the spices in the salami, the oyster's musky oil, the clean sharp orange peel when I break it. I can smell the rock, knowing as I do that these are not his memories, or even finally mine, but only words.

~

The plaid flannel shirt I took from his last closet is one of many I gave him – a "really good shirt," he called it. Over many washings, even as it softened, it kept its bright ground, the color of an apple flying not on a branch but in the mind's eye. Far too big for me (he was over six foot; I'm just over five), the shirt is good for throwing on over a t-shirt on a cold night. Though of course I've washed it, I imagine I still smell him in its weave.

Maybe he imagined one of his sons would take it, if he imagined anything in his last diminishing year. We may "assign" our "portions" as we wish; we can't control where they go. I've gazed online, never in person, at a small auburn curl from Emily Dickinson's twenty-three-year-old head, now owned by Amherst College, which received it from the descendants of her lifelong friend Emily Fowler (Ford). Dickinson's letter said, "I shall never give you anything again that will be half so full of sunshine as this wee lock of hair, but I wish no hue more sombre might ever fall to you."

According to the journalist Steven Slosberg, two other locks listed as Dickinson's were left in the estate of the poet J.D. McClatchy. They are of different colors, only one the vibrant auburn she was known for in her youth, but whose hair stays the same? Together, they sold at auction for $800, despite the uncertainties of their provenance, or because of them. The locks came to McClatchy on the death of his friend James Merrill. Nobody is saying for sure how Merrill got them, but when Slosberg sent an inquiry to Langdon Hammer, author of the 2015 biography *James Merrill: Life and Art*, Hammer wrote back with "a story about JM breaking into the Dickinson house with some friends and making off with some goods. He said he took, if memory serves, a sherry glass — in honor of her eyes (which she described as sherry-colored). I assumed," Hammer continues, "this was an apocryphal story. But the Dickinson scholar Ralph Franklin suspects JM did in fact break in — perhaps to the Gables? Dickinson's brother-in-law's house. How else to explain the copy of Dickinson's poems inscribed to her sister-in-law Susan Gilbert, if memory serves, which was in JM's collection, and later donated by Sandy to the Beinecke."

Sherry glasses. Sherry-colored eyes. A book inscribed – by whom, since Dickinson herself was dead before any collection of her poems came out? – to the woman she may have loved above all others, to whom she wrote frequent passionate letters, even while Susan lived next door. Light as apples, her letters, or bees, ornamented with her barely legible hand; magic, the hand-stitched fascicles; more magic still, the poems she wrote on the backs of envelopes: her script curving around flaps and addresses, the occasional whimsy of an additional fragment pinned on.

3.

Since the virus came, except when I'm running or performing essential errands, I find myself inside my glass box, spinning with my things through space. "Now is a gift of the gods and an access into reality," Anne Carson tells us, though just at the moment, in our endless indoor wheel-spinning out of the present, I find it difficult to believe her.

To Dickinson, bees are never superfluous. Nothing is, especially not *now*. She never meant me "to make a prairie," least of all in our lifetimes.

Maybe when she wrote she imagined someone like my father, who, when I was a child, planted trees that now tower over the neighborhood. Even when those trees had grown to the eaves, he decided the beech was a little too close to the house, so grabbed his shovel and drove his truck onto the lawn, full of purpose and joy – not to remove the tree, but to move it a few feet over – drawing the neighbors out to watch and comment.

Dickinson may have meant him, or me, or someone else in this future she either could or couldn't have imagined, to make or read a poem. Likely, she didn't care what any of us might do.

Except that when her sister threw open the trunk, looking for Emily's letters to burn as instructed, she found, to her astonishment, almost 2000 poems. Which, Emily not having mentioned them in her instructions, Lavinia had the sense not to burn.

Like the poet, a bee works and works again over her blossom, gathering and stuffing her little thigh-pouches until it seems impossible she might still fly. The blossom keeps yielding, and between bee and flower I am entirely carried away, flying at once like an apple leaving orbit and like a bee loaded down. The poem has found and instructed me, as it tells me in its last turn, not in agri- or apiculture but in "revery," in the making of a dream of clover over which a bee in her singular resonant multitude browses, as do I. Conjured objects, and revered – clover, apple, bee – release me into the dreaming field of poetry, and this is the poem's instruction.

When I first read "To make a prairie," I assumed the clover flower was pinkish-white, like the clover I see in my yard. But prairie clover is gorgeously purple, something my father would have known. The poem doesn't care either way. You don't have to *see* any of it. Rather, Dickinson depends on your apprehending.

The objects are everything. And, like so many things, also beside the point.

Dickinson eludes us because she means to.

"Neither for me honey nor the honey bee," says Carson's Sappho. And yet, between them, Sappho and Carson, like Dickinson, give us both.

~

Aside from his lutes and red flannel shirt, the objects that came to me from my father came before he died, though after he had begun his long passing away. When he went into care, my mother sold the family home and its veranda, its high ceilings and commensurately long staircases, including the wooden one, polished to a treacherous shine and bottoming out at a hard marble floor. What she didn't take with her to her new condo she offered to her children. What we didn't want, and a few things we did, she gave away or sold, more or less ruthlessly.

I had no use for my father's hunting rifles or place for the excellent canoe my mother bought him one birthday. His little bits of jewelry and cashmere sweaters, which like his best wines he saved for festive occasions, went to my brothers, the cellar to my mother, who shares it with her children a few bottles at a time.

In truth, my father never collected ornaments and baubles, though I happily wear my great-grandmother's passed-down jewels with jeans and flannel, as if they are meant for real life. He, too, liked things he could use: bungee cords, his instruments, good knives, cameras and binoculars; trucks with the power to uproot mature trees; the Mojo Pizza ballcap my older brother brought him from Phoenix, or the one I carried back from Palmer Station in Antarctica, which let him bear an applique of a frozen continent like a hood ornament on his forehead. A fan of magpies, a Depression baby, my father repurposed yogurt containers and collected used twist-ties, tinfoil re-smoothed and folded away in a drawer. He might say of a paper sack that looked binnable but whose structural integrity he'd assessed at a touch, "That's a really good bag." When his children made fun of him, he would say, wearing his serious face over his satirical one, "In the next war, you'll come begging for rubber bands."

"If you really get down to the disaster, the slightest eloquence becomes unbearable," Beckett says.

The next war, or something like it, has arrived, and keeps arriving. His rubber bands are gone.

~

After he died, of course, people told me things about him I wished I'd always known. He had taught my mother to see animals that were secreted, invisible to others, in their environments: fawns left safely nestled among leaves (my father could smell them, she said); leaf-shaped birds sheltering in the trees. He once sat in a winter clearing and hushed an old friend, the friend told me, so they could hear snowflakes crackling. I have their stories and my own that, like some objects, keep coming to mind. I mean "come" in the sense of rise, into clarity, into semblance and resonance.

Carson says, "In any act of thinking the mind must reach across this space between known and unknown, linking one to the other but also keeping visible their difference."

Where go we? I wonder now if I should have taken a lock of hair, some clippings from his fingernails. It would have been unlike me a year ago, but now, so many others having slipped alone into memory, I might become a person who would wear a piece of her dead father in a locket.

"The tie between us is very fine," Dickinson wrote to Susan Gilbert, "but a hair never dissolves."

At night, the bright outside fades from my rooms.

My house, its ghostly interior reflected on itself again and again, overflows its objects.

The body I hardly notice any more glimmers faintly by.

Sources

Ammons, A.R. *The Complete Poems of A.R. Ammons, Volume 2* 1928-2005 (Robert M. West, ed.). New York: WW Norton, 2017.

Ashbery, John. *Self-Portrait in a Convex Mirror*. New York: Penguin Books, 1972.

Barzun, Jacques. "The Paradoxes of Creativity." *The American Scholar*, Vol. 58, No. 3 (Summer 1989), pp. 337-351.

Berssenbrugge, Mei-mei. *Hello, the Roses*. New York: New Directions, 2013.

Bowles, Nellie. "Custodian of the Patriarchy." *New York Times*, May 18, 2018. https://www.nytimes.com/2018/05/18/style/jordan-peterson-12-rules-for-life.html. Accessed, May 2018.

Bryan, Sharon. "Use Capricious in a Sentence." *Salt Air*. Middletown, CT: Wesleyan University Press, 1983.

Calvino, Italo. *Invisible Cities*. New York: Harcourt, Brace, Jovanovich, 1978.

Calvino, Italo. *Marcovaldo: Or Seasons in the City*. New York: Mariner Books, 1983.

Carson, Anne. *Eros the Bittersweet*. New York: Dalkey Archive Press, 1998.

Carson, Anne, translator. *If Not Winter: Fragments of Sappho*. New York: Vintage, 2013.

Coles, Katharine. "Good Eye." *Fault*. Los Angeles: Red Hen Press, 2008.

--. "At Pompeii." *Flight*. Los Angeles: Red Hen Press, 2016.

Czamecki, Marek. "Blessed Virgin Mary, Helper in Childbirth." Our Lady of Guadalupe Chapel, Franciscan

Friars of the Immaculate. https://figuadalupe.files.wordpress.com/2011/01/helperinbirth-small.jpg.

Dickinson, Emily. "A narrow fellow in the Grass," F1096, J986. *Emily Dickinson Archive*. https://www.edickinson.org/editions/1/image_sets/236315. Transcribed by author.

--. "A spider sewed at night," F1163/J1138. *Emily Dickinson Archive*. https://www.edickinson.org/editions/1/image_sets/12176929. Transcribed by author.

--. "After great pain," F372a, J341. *Emily Dickinson Archive*. https://www.edickinson.org/editions/1/image_sets/235652. Transcribed by author.

--. "Death sets a Thing significant," J360. *Emily Dickinson Archive*. https://www.edickinson.org/editions/2/image_sets/75346. Transcribed by author.

--. "He fumbles at your soul." J3154, Fr477. *Emily Dickinson Archive*. http://www.edickinson.org/editions/1/image_sets/237002. Transcribed by author.

--. "His Feet are shod with Gauze." F979A, J916. *Emily Dickinson Archive*. https://www.edickinson.org/editions/1/image_sets/236389. Transcribed by author.

--. "'Hope is the thing with feathers." J254/F314. *Emily Dickinson Archive*. https://www.edickinson.org/editions/2/image_sets/12169613. Transcribed by author.

--. "How human nature dotes," F1440A/J1417. *Emily Dickinson Archive*. *https://www.edickinson.org/editions/1/image_sets/239594*. Transcribed by author.

--. "I felt a cleaving in my mind." F867a, J937. *Emily Dickinson Archive*. https://www.edickinson.org/editions/1/image_sets/237400. Transcribed by author.

--. "I found the words to every thought." J581, F436. *Emily Dickinson Archive*. http://www.edickinson.org/editions/1/image_sets/235598. Transcribed by author.

--. "I had not minded walls. J398/F554. *Emily Dickinson Archive*. https://www.edickinson.org/editions/2/image_sets/12169969. Transcribed by author.

--. "I heard a fly buzz – when I died." F591A/J465. *Emily Dickinson Archive. https://www.edickinson.org/editions/1/image_sets/235826*. Transcribed by author.

--. "I Never Hear that One Is Dead." F1325, J1323. *Emily Dickinson Archive*. https://www.edickinson.org/editions/1/image_sets/239130. Transcribed by author.

--. Letter #271, to Thomas Higginson. *Emily Dickinson Archive*. http://archive.emilydickinson.org/correspondence/higginson/l271.html.

--. Letter to Emily Fowler Ford, *Dickinson/Ford Correspondence. Emily Dickinson Archive*. http://archive.emilydickinson.org/correspondence/ford/l99.html.

--. Letter to Susan Gilbert. *Correspondence with Susan Gilbert. Emily Dickinson Archive*. http://archive.emilydickinson.org/working/zhb148b.htm.

--. "Long years apart." J1383/F1405A. *Emily Dickinson Archive. https://www.edickinson.org/editions/2/image_sets/12172350*. Transcribed by author.

--. "Tell all the truth." F1263/J1129. *Emily Dickinson Archive. https://www.edickinson.org/editions/1/image_sets/238526* . Transcribed by author.

--. "The love a life can show below," F285/J673. *Emily Dickinson Archive*. https://www.edickinson.org/editions/1/image_sets/236056. Transcribed by author.

--. "The spider holds a silver ball," F513/J605. *Emily Dickinson Archive*. https://www.edickinson.org/editions/1/image_sets/235783. Transcribed by author.

--. "'Tis a single hair," F554/J398. *Emily Dickinson Archive*. https://www.edickinson.org/editions/1/image_sets/236056. Transcribed by author.

--. "To be alive is power." F876/J677. *Emily Dickinson Archive*. https://www.edickinson.org/editions/1/image_sets/237461. Transcribed by author.

--. "To make a prairie." J1755/F1779. *The Poems of Emily Dickinson*. Ralph W. Franklin, ed.
Cambridge, The Belnap Press, 1998. Text first published 1896, Todd and Bianci series.

--. "We Fit Our Vision to the Dark." F428a, J419. *Emily Dickinson Archive*. https://www.edickinson.org/editions/2/image_sets/74974. Transcribed by author.

Dictionary.com. https://www.dictionary.com/browse/brute. December, 2019.

--. Dictionary.com. https://www.dictionary.com/browse/rogue. December, 2019.

Eliot, T.S. "The Wasteland." *The Poetry Foundation*. https://www.poetryfoundation.org/poems/47311/the-waste-land.

Fabrizio, Doug. Host and interviewer. *Radio West*. http://radiowest.kuer.org/post/conversation-katharine-coles. April 4, 2016.

--. Intelligence in the Flesh (conversation with Guy Claxton). July 1, 2016. https://radiowest.kuer.org/post/intelligence-flesh-1.

Forbush, E.H. and May. *Natural History of the Birds of Eastern and Central North America*. Boston: Houghton, 1939.

Frost, Robert. "Fire and Ice." https://www.poetryfoundation.org/poems/44263/fire-and-ice.

Francesca, Piero. *Madonna del Parto*. https://it.wikipedia.org/wiki/Madonna_del_Parto#/media/File:Madonna_del_parto_pierodella_Francesca.jpg.

Fulton, Alice. Audio interview with A.R. Ammons. *Poets in Person*, Poetry magazine. Transcribed by
Katharine Coles, April 2019.

Graham, Jorie. "Prayer." *Never*. New York: HarperCollins, 2002. https://www.poetryfoundation.org/poems/47197/prayer-56d2277b19acb.

--. "San Sepolchro." *Dream of the Unified Field*. New York: Ecco, 1997. https://www.poetryfoundation.org/poems/47184/san-sepolcro.

Hopkins, Gerard Manley. "Spring and Fall." https://www.poetryfoundation.org/poems/44400/spring-and-fall.

Johnson, Lynn. Tribune staff photographer. *Salt Lake Tribune*. April 8, 1968.

Johnson, Thomas H., ed. *Emily Dickinson, Selected Letters*. Cambridge, MA: The Belknap Press, 1958.

Keats, John. Letter #22, to John Bailey. https://ebooks.adelaide.edu.au/k/keats/john/letters/letter22.html

--. Letter #24, to George and Thomas Keats. https://ebooks.adelaide.edu.au/k/keats/john/letters/letter24.html.

--. Letter #76, to Richard Woodhouse. https://ebooks.adelaide.edu.au/k/keats/john/letters/letter76.html.

--. "Ode on Melancholy." https://www.poetryfoundation.org/poems/44478/ode-on-melancholy.

--. "Ode on a Grecian Urn." https://www.poetryfoundation.org/poems/44477/ode-on-a-grecian urn.

Lawrence, D.H. *St. Mawr. The Short Novels, vol. 2*. London: William Heinemann, LTD, 1915.

Leigh-Holt, Allison. Artist Statement, *The Glass System*. https://www.ndmoa.com/past-2016-allison-holt.

Parmagianino, *Self Portrait in a Convex Mirror*. https://en.wikipedia.org/wiki/Self-portrait_in_a_Convex_Mirror#/media/File:Parmigianino_Selfportrait.jpg.

Perry, Sarah. *The Essex Serpent*. New York: Custom House, 2017.

Rekdal, Paisley. "Four Marys." *Nightingale*. Port Townsend, WA: Copper Canyon Press, 2019.

Rich, Adrienne. "Planetarium." *Collected Poems*. New York: W.W. Norton, 2016.

Shackleton, Ernest. *South*. Melbourne, AU: Text Publishing, 1919.

Slosberg, Steven. "The Bewildering Provenance of Emily Dickinson's Auburn Locks." *The Westerly Sun*, May 25, 2019. https://www.thewesterlysun.com/opinion/guest-columns/postscripts-the-bewildering-provenance-of-emily-dickinson-s-auburn-locks/article_4704226e-7eb5-11e9-9e9c-dfc674af5052.html.

Spies, Walter. Starfish detail. https://www.liveauctioneers.com/item/20632100_walter-spies-1895-1942-watercolour-detailed.

Van Eyck, Jan. *The Arnolfini Portrait*. The National Gallery, London. https://en.wikipedia.org/wiki/Arnolfini_Portrait#/media/File:Van_Eyck_Arnolfini_Portrait.jpg

---. *Annunciation*. National Gallery of Art, Washington, D.C. https://www.nga.gov/collection/art-object-page.46.html

Webster, John. *The Duchess of Malfi*. https://www.gutenberg.org/files/2232/2232-h/2232-h.htm.

Whitman, Walt. "A Noiseless Patient Spider." https://poets.org/poem/noiseless-patient-spider.

Whyte, David. Conversation with Krista Tippett. https://onbeing.org/programs/david-whyte-the-conversational-nature-of-reality-dec2018/.

Williams, William Carlos. *Selected Essays of William Carlos Williams*. New York: New Directions, 1969.

Wikipedia. https://en.wikipedia.org/wiki/Lens_(anatomy). Accessed June-July, 2017.

Yeats, W.B. "The Second Coming." *The Poetry Foundation*. www.poetryfoundation.org.

Permissions

Company, LLC on behalf of Copper Canyon Press, coppercanyonpress.org.

Excerpts from "Use Capricious in a Sentence" are from *Salt Air* by Sharon Bryan. Copyright ©1983 by Sharon Bryan. Used by permission of the author.

The author gratefully acknowledges the Emily Dickinson Archive, an open source website through which a number of libraries and institutions have made many of Dickinson's original handwritten poems and other materials available in facsimile for the use of scholars. Having access to this material changed my relationship to and understanding of Dickinson's work.

Acknowledgments

So many people have encouraged and supported the writing in this book, and so many unnamed friends and loved ones haunt its pages, that it's impossible to thank them all. However, in addition to my fabulous editor and publisher, Ruth Greenstein, and my friend and copy editor, Wyn Cooper, I would like to extend particular thanks to Scott Black, Kay Winder, Paul Hetherington, Jen Webb, Graeme Harper, Shane Strange, Andrew Melrose, Paul Munden, Maureen O'Hara Ure, and, especially and always, Melanie Rae Thon and Chris Johnson, all of whom remind me constantly of the seamlessness between love and work.

About the Author

Katharine Coles is the author of two novels, seven collections of poems, and the memoir *Look Both Ways*. The recipient of grants from the NEA, the NEH, and the Guggenheim Foundation, she has served as Poet Laureate of Utah and was inaugural director of the Poetry Foundation's Harriet Monroe Poetry Institute. She is a distinguished professor of English at the University of Utah.